Put Your Life on a Diet

GREGORY PAUL JOHNSON

Put Your Life On a Diet

LESSONS LEARNED FROM LIVING IN 140 SQUARE FEET

GIBBS SMITH

TO ENRICH AND INSPIRE HUMANKIND

Salt Lake City | Charleston | Santa Fe | Santa Barbara

First Edition
12 11 10 09 08   5 4 3 2 1

Text © 2008 Gregory Paul Johnson

Published by
Gibbs Smith
P.O. Box 667
Layton, Utah 84041

Orders: 1.800.835.4993
gibbs-smith.com

Cover designed by Ryan Christopher
Interior pages designed by Kurt Wahlner
Printed and bound in the U.S.

Library of Congress Cataloging-in-Publication Data

Johnson, Gregory P. (Gregory Paul), 1961-
  Put your life on a diet : lessons learned from living in 140 square feet /
Gregory Johnson. — 1st ed.
      p. cm.
  ISBN-13: 978-1-4236-0317-7
  ISBN-10: 1-4236-0317-6
  1. Simplicity. 2. Small houses. 3. Personal space. 4. Life skills. 5.
Sustainable living. I. Title.
  TX147.J638 2008
  643'.1—dc22
                              2008007919

Dedicated to our shared future—a future of hope, progress, cooperation, enlightenment, and transcendence.

ACKNOWLEDGMENTS

There are many people I wish to thank for assisting in the writing of this book. I first want to thank Gibbs Smith, Publisher, for providing valuable input, expertise, and support for the writing, layout, publishing, and promotion of the book. I'm grateful to Jay Shafer, who helped take me to the next level of smaller and simpler living. I want to thank my family, friends, advisory board, colleagues, and clients for their support along the way. In particular, I want to thank my dad, Nicholas Johnson, who, in 1972, wrote the book *Test Pattern for Living*, which inspired me to live a more conscientious and mindful life. Last, but certainly not least, I am grateful to God for inspiration, vision, wisdom, and strength.

CONTENTS

Introduction: A Simple Approach to Better Living 9

1 How Ready Are You to Slim Down Your Life? 15

2 Your Health and the Health of the Planet 29

3 Cutting Calories from Your Livable Space 47

4 How Green Is Your Home? 63

5 Traveling Green 85

6 Technology Is Shrinking Our Lives 99

7 How Small Will You Go? 117

Resources for Simple Living 131

Introduction

A Simple Approach to Better Living

As you simplify your life, the laws of the universe will be simpler; solitude will not be solitude; poverty will not be poverty; nor weakness, weakness.

—Henry David Thoreau

I LIVE in a home of 140 square feet. It doesn't have a furnace, air conditioner, refrigerator, dishwasher, clothes washer/dryer, vacuum cleaner, blender, disposal, trash compactor, or other home appliances. For most of my commuting, I walk or rely on a bicycle year-round rather than a car. My small home is completely off the electrical and water grids. Most people would say that this is an impossible way to live, but the truth is, my transition to a simpler life has made me happier and healthier than I have ever been.

When we come to a certain way of thinking and living, it is usually a result of many experiences and encounters throughout life that shape us along the way. So it is with my interest in smaller living. Since I was very young, I have always had a fascination with the idea of having an efficiently designed small home. In 2001, I saw an article in the *Des Moines Register* about Jay Shafer, who at the time was living in a 10 x 14-foot home he built on a trailer. The home was constructed using residential-grade materials and insulation for economical year-round habitation—something that most RVs and camper trailers lack since they are usually designed for seasonal part-time use. This fusion of camper and house intrigued me. I contacted the *Des Moines Register* to get approval for putting a copy of the article on my Web site with other related simple and small living resources.

BY 2002, I began receiving e-mails and phone calls from people who had seen the article about Jay Shafer on my Web site. I eventually came into contact with him, and he was delighted to learn of my interest in his home. In the fall of 2002, Jay invited me to attend a presentation at the Iowa City Public Library on small and alternative homes. While I did not own a small or alternative home at the time, I was still very interested in that unique way of living. I was impressed by the presentation, and at the end of the meeting, I commented that someone should start an organization in response to the small house movement. Jay and the others at the meeting laughed and said that during dinner they had been discussing that very same idea and thought I would be just the person to start such an organization. They were already familiar with some of the work I had done through my ResourcesforLife.com Web site. So, the next day we put together the initial modest Web page and the Small House Society was born. Originally, I was "elected" as the leader since I would be taking on the bulk of e-mails, phone calls, correspondence, expenses, and maintenance of the Web site.

By 2003, I had reached a point in my life where I needed a change. It didn't make sense to rent a small apartment, never putting money toward owning a home. I imagined thirty years down the road having spent thousands of dollars on rent with nothing to show for it. Once I stopped and thought about where my money was going, I began looking at my options for purchasing a small house or condo. What I discovered is that, while efficiency apartments exist, efficiency condos are not as readily available. Local housing codes have made it illegal to build a small "efficiency house," deeming such a dwelling uninhabitable even though an equivalent dwelling as an apartment is legal. Basically what I wanted was the option to own a simple room like the one I was currently renting. The solution was obvious. Not only was I impressed with people like Jay who live in compact, environmentally friendly homes, but I was also the head of the Small House Society. I felt strongly that it was important to be part of the small house community and reduce my environmental footprint. I worked closely with Jay Shafer on the custom design of my house plans, and within three months my home was built.

While living in my compact home for the last several years, I have learned that as my living space became smaller, my freedom expanded both in terms of finances and free time. This increase in time and money has impacted every area of my life. Eventually I lost about a hundred pounds, after having been overweight for almost a decade. The weight loss was the result of working less, sleeping more, having more time to exercise, and replacing my car with a bike. I also now have extra money to join a gym and make healthier eating choices. Having more time and money allows me to give more of myself to family and friends. I've been able to expand my volunteer time and financial donations to causes I believe in. My career has deepened and expanded, because I've been able to focus on professional development and pursue opportunities for growth. Rather than worry about short-term financial needs, I've been able to pursue those things that promise long-term benefits.

What excites me most about simple living is how micro decisions can have a macro impact. For me, building and living in a smaller home has resulted in a significantly reduced cost of living; my home's cost of construction, utility bills, and maintenance are much lower than the costs for an average home. Living in a smaller space also puts a limit on my purchases, thus saving me money. All of these factors result in having a smaller environmental footprint, which benefits everyone.

While living in a home of 140 square feet, I find that I am still using about two thousand square feet of space, just as I had in the past. The difference is that the other 1,860 square feet that comprise my office, the gym, the laundromat, restaurants, and other spaces are not mine to maintain anymore—they are shared with others. So not only am I contributing to my community, but my overhead and responsibilities have been significantly reduced. In our complex and busy world, many people are searching for a simpler life, like prospectors panning for an elusive gold nugget. It was, in fact, the act of getting rid of my possessions that allowed me to obtain the treasure of simplicity.

This book is not only a record of my journey toward simpler living but also what I have learned on the way that can help you simplify your life. I don't expect that most people will make the extreme choice I did, but who doesn't want a life that's simply satisfying, simply fulfilling, and simply great? I put my life on a new path and changed everything for the better. Let me help you start on your path, too.

Gregory Paul Johnson
Iowa City, Iowa, USA

Put Your Life on a Diet

1

How Ready Are You to Slim Down Your Life?

> You must be
> the change you
> wish to see in
> the world.
>
> —Mahatma Gandhi

Where I Was

MY TRANSITION to a simpler life was partly by choice and also by circumstance. By the year 2000, I was divorced, overweight, and living in a 120-square-foot room that I was renting in an older home. Most of my possessions were in a climate-controlled storage facility, and I kept only what I needed on a daily basis in my living space. I wasn't ready to part with my possessions, but it was more economical to keep them in storage rather than find a larger apartment to put them in. I worked as a consultant, so most of my time was spent in my room or on the road doing client work. Since I was increasingly working in the information world of the Internet, there was much I could do from home. Like many people, by the end of the day my time and energy were exhausted, and I didn't feel like I was contributing much to my personal growth, society, or the environment. I began the search for change.

One aspect of smaller and simpler living involves the basic element of designing an effective and efficient living space. However, it isn't enough to simply move into a smaller physical living space; it's also necessary to "remodel" oneself on the inside. For all of us, our first home is the body we live in. For this reason, to live a simpler life one should do the inner work necessary to find pleasure, joy, and meaning in a smaller and simpler space. Being content in your first home (the body) is essential to finding contentment in your second home (the house you live in). This is an internal work that nobody else can really do for you.

I began paying more attention to my health and keeping track of how I was spending my time and money. I needed to understand how I was dissatisfied with my life in order to figure out how to change it. Keeping track of my priorities helped me see where I had been and where I was going. Any area of life you begin to track, you can control.

Gaining self-awareness, self-control, and self-discipline in my struggle with weight loss helped me in other areas of my life, and I was then able to thoughtfully map out my journey toward simplicity.

Where I Am Now

The small steps that you take to change your life can have the greatest long-term impact. For me, this was literally true. Having gone from a home of about 2,000 square feet, at first I found it difficult to live in the cramped quarters of my rented room, but over the next few years I lived in several efficiency-size rentals and soon grew to value the simplicity of having a sparse home. It became easier to distance myself from my possessions that were still sitting untouched in a storage facility, because I realized I didn't need them. Living in a small room prevented me from spending money on items I didn't really need.

In the year 2003, I took the most significant step on my journey to simplifying my life.

I decided to move into an off-the-grid house of 140 square feet.

I did this not only for my personal improvement, but also because I care deeply about how I affect the world around me. Moving into a space that small as a permanent home forced me to streamline many of my routines and habits, and my life has changed dramatically. Let me give you an example of my daily routine.

I usually go to sleep around 9 p.m. and wake up around 5 a.m. After a brief stretching exercise (similar to yoga or Pilates) and a quiet meditation, I go directly to the gym where I use the restroom facilities, shower, shave, and get dressed for my workday. I am able to enjoy the beauty of nature because my bicycle is my main means of transportation. I enjoy spending time consulting and doing volunteer work rather than just sitting at home. By the time I do get home in the evening, it is usually time for bed. If I am traveling or staying at someone's home, going running outdoors and using resistance bands indoors for strength training can replace the gym.

Living a more simple life allows me to wake up excited for each day, and when the day's over, I am fulfilled by how I live. The reason for this is because I start each day with less "weight" on my shoulders. With additional energy and less clutter in my life, I have become more productive with my day job and my consulting business, and I am able to contribute to the community. I feel healthy and happy. Economically, I'm like someone who earns a nice salary in the United States and then lives on that salary in a developing nation. I spend money frugally. Instead of trying to live on my full income, I have a lifestyle that can be sustained on about half of what I'm earning. By contrast, many people today are living on 105 percent of their income, going further into debt each month. My system creates a comfortable gap between my lifestyle and my income.

I also wanted to improve the environment with my home choice. I wanted to make a difference and become more conscientious about how I treated the earth. I have been a long-time activist, but I was often discouraged at not being able to do more. I had the attitude that I was only one person and how could one person make a difference? I eventually realized that living the answer would accomplish more than protesting, shouting, or carrying a picket sign.

My answer was "lifestyle activism."

I knew that others might copy my example of responsible living, and the domino effect could produce significant positive results. I am glad to say that my small home has done exactly that. By living in a smaller space and utilizing public or commercial spaces more, it is possible to utilize resources (such as heat and lighting) that are already being expended. For example, a public library will have heat and lighting all day whether fifty people use the facility or one hundred people. However, within a home, the use of lights and heat are often determined by when people are there.

Start Your Life Diet

The journey toward simplification will be different for every person, because decisions are based upon individual priorities and callings in life. Your path will be different than your neighbor's or mine, but starting on your path and staying there is what is important. In this book I am going to focus on five major areas where I was able to simplify and slim down my life: health, livable space utilization, utilities, transportation, and technology.

However, before we start looking at the solutions, we need to start identifying the problems. Start with an internal evaluation of what your life is like now, just as I had to do. After you identify problem areas, you can go about changing them. Simply put, once you've eliminated the short-term crisis situations in your life, you can begin to plan and live proactively with the long term in mind. What you need to remember is that you will be starting with small changes.

Having an "all or nothing" mentality will prevent you from exploring the benefits of making smaller compromises for the better.

A compromising change that you commit to over a long period of time is of more benefit than the dramatic change you don't stick with or even make because it is so extreme.

Below I am going to ask you several questions to get you thinking about what your life is like now and how you might want to change it. At the end of this chapter you are going to have room to jot down your answers. As you read through these questions, take the time to write down your thoughts so that you can reference them later on.

Time and Money

Before I go into the areas of change, I want to talk briefly about time and money. If we all get twenty-four hours in a day, how is it that some people seem to get so much more accomplished? How is it that they also seem to be able to afford more than others? I've heard it said that you can tell a lot about people's priorities by examining how they spend their time and money.

Your Average Day
Should Reflect Your Priorities

Number these eight categories in their order of importance in your life as they are now and as you would like them to be—1 is most important and 8 is least important.

	How they are now	How I want them to be
Religious/Spiritual		
Family		
Entertainment		
Marriage		
Friends		
Health		
Career		
Community		

Understanding your priorities will help you schedule your time. Most areas of life are interdependent. If you make a commitment to regular exercise and professional career growth, your health and financial well-being are stronger. Having these areas of life in good shape will make a person more available to family and friends. In this way, health maintenance and career growth are prerequisite foundational priorities to family and friends. Sometimes those things in life that seem to be lower priorities can serve higher priorities. Many people let life happen to them and then they react, instead of planning in advance and taking care of small problems before they get out of control. Crisis situations seem to happen at the worst possible time and often take much more effort, energy, and resources than simple life-maintenance tasks. One principle of effective time budgeting is to be proactive and preventative. Consider the following:

- How efficient are you at multitasking?
- Do you plan errands weekly and map your route so that you will save the greatest amount of time on the road?

- How much time do you spend watching television or surfing the Internet?
- Do you plan ahead on how you will spend your day or weekend?

How you rate your priorities not only affects your time but your money as well. Statistics on consumer debt suggest that many people spend a large amount of their budget on retail consumer goods and consumables that are rapidly depreciating. The act of "trying to get rich" or at least look wealthy is the very mindset that traps people into a life of poverty. This may result from purchasing items way beyond your means in order to look successful or by running up a credit card balance for material things that you don't really need. On the other hand, some people, out of shortsightedness or imagined frugality, purchase the least expensive item rather than purchase the least expensive item to own and maintain. More often than not, the least expensive item will break down along the way and have to be replaced, costing you more than if you'd invested in a quality item.

By simplifying your life and focusing on your priorities, it is possible to dramatically increase your monthly disposable income. What would you do with an extra $300, $500, or $1,200 per month? Pay off all your bills? Go back to school? Invest in a profitable business? Consider the following:

- Where does the bulk of your money go each month?
- Do you have a monthly budget written down?
- How often do you stay within your budget?
- How often do you buy impulsively instead of plan purchases in advance?
- Do you shop from a prioritized "wish list" of items you have wanted for a long time?

A person with desires that exceed their means will forever be in a state of lack. They will be poor no matter how much money they have. Take the time to align your priorities with your spending habits. With creativity, planning, and forethought it is possible to dramatically reduce your "needs" by living more efficiently. The basic needs remain the same (food, clothing, shelter) yet what's required to meet those needs is reduced.

So, as you consider your time and financial expenditures, even the smallest decisions and expenditures toward your priorities can help build a better life. Simplifying your life involves planning and thinking ahead.

Health

Your health impacts every aspect of your life including the environment around you. It is not solely about what you eat but also your commitment to exercise, to meditate, and to develop your spiritual well-being. Consider the following:

- How healthy do you feel on a day-to-day basis?
- How long has it been since your last medical checkup?
- Do you pay attention to nutritional content and do you exercise regularly?
- Do you feel like you should be recycling more than you are?
- Do you keep harmful chemicals around that may damage your health and the environment?

Livable Space Utilization

Some people fall into the trap of thinking that a larger house will cure their over-crowded-home syndrome. This is similar to thinking that going on a crash diet to lose ten pounds will solve weight problems over the long run. When people lose weight quickly without making permanent lifestyle changes to their diet and exercise, they typically gain the weight back. People who receive large financial windfalls may pay off their existing bills and debts, yet soon they have the same financial problems they had before. The same goes for selecting a bigger house. The problem may not be how much room you have, but how you utilize that space. Living within the boundaries of our physical space is like living within the boundaries of our financial income. The discipline and self-control required is the same for these two areas of life.

When people move into a bigger house without examining their purchasing habits (or hoarding habits), the bigger house will simply fill up with stuff, and they'll feel cramped again. For such people, no amount of space is ever enough. Contentment inside can change how we feel about all the things on the outside. Consider the following in your own situation:

- How long do you see yourself living in your present home?
- What are the aspects of your home that you do like?
- What are the aspects of your home that you don't like?
- Is it the actual design of your home or the clutter inside that is the problem?
- If clutter is the problem, do you need help changing your pack rat mentality?

When the day is over, I am fulfilled by how I live . . . because I start each day with less "weight" on my shoulders.

Utilities

Sometimes we may not realize how much of our time and money is spent on the utilities and upkeep of our home. In turn, we may not be aware of how our energy consumption affects the environment. Consider the following:

- What percent of you budget goes toward housing (mortgage, insurance, utilities, taxes, etc.)?
- Are your gas, electricity, and water bills steadily increasing?
- Are you actively trying to save energy?
- How large is your environmental footprint?
- How environmentally friendly are the materials within your home?

Transportation

Where you live and work affects your mode of transportation. Not only do you need your commute or trips to the grocery store to be efficient, but you also need to be aware of how your habits affect the environment. Consider the following:

- Do you own a car?
- How often do you waste gas on inefficiently planned trips?
- Are there times when you can walk or ride a bike to complete an errand?
- Is public transportation available for long commutes?
- Are you open to carpooling or ridesharing? Why or why not?

Technology

We live in a digital society. Technology affects everything in our lives and will only increase its effect as time passes. Consider the following:

- Are you utilizing technology to make your life simpler?
- Have you distinguished between technology that makes your life simpler and those gadgets which take away from your life by consuming your time and money?
- Are you intimidated by technology?
- Are you willing to take classes and learn to be more effective with the resources available to you?
- Do you continually upgrade your equipment, or is what you have adequate for your needs?
- Do you recycle old technology?

You can change your life and make a positive impact on the environment. Change is never easy, but taking small steps will help you move in the right direction. At each chapter's conclusion, there will be a series of action points and discussion questions, and a planning section. The action points are key ideas from the chapter to encourage you to make changes. Select one or two to work on at a time. The discussion questions allow you to bring others into the journey with you.

Everyone needs a support system, and talking with others makes you more accountable for your goals.

Your support group can also cheer you on when you feel overwhelmed. They can provide you with feedback and creative solutions to challenges you are facing. For the planning section, you will have a blank page ir two to write down your thoughts and goals as you read this book.

PERSONALIZE THIS BOOK. Let it be part journal, part diary, and part worksheet. The ideas I suggest and the ones found in your own mind and heart should hopefully turn into positive action. What will you do because of what you've read? I'd love to hear from you about your own journey and experiences. Feel free to contact me and chat with others about the issues raised in this book. To do so, you can visit the ResourcesforLife.com Web site. We are all in this together, and if I can do it, you can definitely do it too.

Action Points

The following action points are things you can do to implement the information shared in this chapter and put your life on a diet. Start today. Begin with one or two action points and slowly implement more as you simplify your life.

1. Make a list of your priorities and keep it in a visible place to remind you how you want to spend your time and money. Keeping these things in your conscious and subconscious will help inspire small and large actions that work toward those ends. Track how you spend your time. Not tracking how you're using your time is like not balancing your checkbook—the chaotic days equate to bounced checks.

2. Commit to making small changes and being mindful of small changes. If you notice that you are slowly gaining weight, accruing debt, or running out of space at home, something needs to be altered. Your corrective action can be smaller (and simpler) if you do so gradually over time. Take time to evaluate your life and make the necessary steps to bring your life back into balance. Choose one thing in your life that is getting out of control and decide today what needs to happen to get it back on track. The skills and discipline you cultivate in this one area can be applied to other areas. The confidence you build by seeing success in one area of life can help you gain victory in other areas.

3. Find balance. Consider the various areas of life that consume most of your time: religious/spiritual, health, career, finances, relationships (marriage/family/friends), and community. Explore more effective ways to handle these areas. By living a balanced life, you become more effective and help enrich the lives of those around you.

4. Think about an important activity in your life. Set aside time for it. Decide what time of day you are going to do it and block that time out in your daily planner. If it requires an investment of money or space, make it. Your commitment to an activity that requires your time, money, and space will result in a higher level of satisfaction.

Discussion Questions

Here are some discussion questions for you, your roommate(s), spouse, family, friends, or book club to consider.

1. Talk with a friend or partner about some of the answers you wrote down for the reflective questions. How ready are you for change and how much help would you need from your support system? Ask if they would be willing to help. Are you willing to help them?

2. Changing your life can be difficult but very rewarding. It takes planning, self-discipline, and hope. Are there people you admire for their strength? Emulate their habits and goals. What has made them who they are today? Remember that change happens one day at a time. Don't get overwhelmed. You can do this.

Your Plan

Now it is your turn to make this chapter yours. Get your thoughts out on paper and make a change! What will you do today to make a difference in your life?

_____

_____

_____

_____

_____

_____

_____

_____

_____

_____

_____

_____

_____

_____

_____

_____

2

Your Health
and
the Health of the Planet

To keep the body in good
health is a duty . . . otherwise
we shall not be able to keep
our mind strong and clear.

—Buddha

AT ONE POINT in my life I was close to one hundred pounds overweight. Not only was my health in serious jeopardy, but I wasn't paying enough attention to how my unhealthy habits were impacting the environment. For example, driving a car all the time was bad for my health and also bad for the health of the planet. Being excessively overweight resulted in back pains and sleepless nights, and I remember when my weight reached over two hundred and ninety pounds. It was at that point, with the three hundred pound signpost ahead, that I decided I had to make a change. My decision was for my own sake as well as for the family, friends, and coworkers who depended on me.

Achieving my fitness goals took several years, and it was through simple changes that the long-term results came.

One benefit of attending to your health is that some living expenses can be reduced. There are significant yet sometimes imperceptible cumulative costs and opportunity costs of having low energy or being foggy-headed and/or sick much of the time. Most people have the desire to eat well and exercise but protest that they haven't set aside the required time and money in their budget. Although exercise takes an investment of time, it also pays back in terms of efficiency. For example, a day's work that might have required sixteen hours may only require twelve hours when you are working with a clearer head and invigorated body. Changing the priorities in your budget each month could make a difference. Early in the day and early in the month, be sure to spend time and money on those things that have the highest priority for you. Nutritious food and a membership to a fitness center (or purchasing workout equipment) may appear to cost more money, but they are investments in your health. The long-term benefits far outweigh the cost. You may also be surprised to find that when you start paying attention to your health, you will be helping the environment as well. Riding a bike is healthy for you and the planet. Eating fresh foods requires less energy to prepare and involves less packaging of foods such as apples, carrots, or bananas.

It Starts With You!

There is an abundance of books, magazines, videos, and other resources that address our nation's insatiable hunger for information about health and wellness. But, in the same way that exercise equipment is sometimes purchased and then gathers dust, health-related materials are often underutilized or completely unused. Many of us are immersed in a flood of nutrition and exercise information, yet where do we begin? Keep in mind that my suggestions for simplifying your health needs are not intended to be used as a regimented diet and exercise guide. If you are serious about improving your health, the first step is deciding that you want to change and are willing to commit to improvement. The next step is to consult a physician so that together you can plan a path to becoming healthy the right way. Finally, start implementing those small changes.

Before we get into nutrition and exercise, I want to briefly mention three important things that have helped me simplify my health needs.

Sleep. It is important to get enough sleep. Sleep habits affect mood, eating habits, metabolism, and energy levels throughout the day. Going to bed early and waking up early can offer many benefits. For example, we're more likely to exercise in the morning if we have the time and energy to do so.

Drink Water. Water is my beverage of choice because I can use the same container over and over for easy refilling. Its production, delivery, storage, and consumption typically require fewer resources and chemicals than dairy products, juices, coffee, or carbonated beverages. Most important of all, getting enough water is essential to helping you stay healthy. Water is good for you and many people don't meet their recommended daily intake, so drink up.

Meditate. One day I read these words on a tea bag, "Meditate by emptying yourself and letting the universe fill you." Personal meditation (especially in the mornings) can help you clear your mind and focus on the positive. These reflective times can be a great source for ideas and creative solutions. It can also give you those few private moments to ponder how you are progressing with your goals. There are many meditation techniques available. What's important is to find one that works for you. A technique I enjoy is quieting my thoughts and ignoring sensory input.

With proper amounts of sleep, adequate hydration, and time for meditation, your journey toward simplifying your overall health needs will be greatly improved, and you may just plain feel better.

Be Wise with Your Calories

When we have money to spend, most of us want to spend it as wisely as possible, getting the most for our money. Similarly, when we eat food, it's a good idea to eat food that is low in calories, high in nutritional value, flavorful, and filling. Awareness and knowledge of what we are eating is essential. Two foods may provide us with the same degree of pleasure, yet one might be very high in calories with little nutritive value while the other is lower in calories with much more nutrition. Knowing this, we can make the better choice. In this way, "dieting" isn't necessarily the practice of choosing bland unsatisfying foods—it's simply the practice of making smarter food choices.

With today's high-calorie foods we can easily exceed our recommended intake, resulting in weight gain. Sometimes we can take out a calorie "loan" from one day to the next, but too many loans produce too many pounds and eventually obesity. Getting control over the persistence of hunger and controlling the amount of calories you consume can help you have better control over other areas in your life.

As you are working on developing your daily calorie budget, you might consider purchasing a body composition monitor and scale such as the one made by Tanita Innerscan. Based on your height, weight, and body composition, these scales can tell you how many calories per day you burn. Body composition monitors will tell you what percentage of your body is fat. So, rather than focusing on losing weight, you can focus your efforts on achieving a healthy level of body fat. Such scales are particularly important for people who are exercising and losing fat but gaining muscle as a result. These scales, depending on the model, can also measure muscle mass, bone mass, and water percentage.

Understanding your nutritional consumption is essential to simplifying your diet.

Remember that old Food Guide Pyramid? Well, the United States Department of Agriculture now sponsors a Web site called mypyramid.gov, which takes the Food Guide Pyramid to a whole new level. This Web site can help you customize your own eating plan for healthy living. Another option is to meet with a nutritionist to ensure that you are getting the right amount of nourishment for your body.

Simple Foods

In my home, I don't have a refrigerator and only recently did I add a small stove. In thinking about a low-impact lifestyle, I decided, at least for my home, to have the foundation of my diet consist mostly of foods that require little preparation and are shelf storable, such as granolas, breads, fruits, crackers, cereals, and other dried goods. Certainly while dining out I can broaden the variety of what I eat.

A strictly vegan or vegetarian diet may feel too restrictive for many people.

Instead, consider making such foods a large portion of your diet, since they typically use less power to grow, harvest, store, and prepare. They are also better for you than many high-calorie preprocessed foods that require more handling and that produce extra waste from their packaging. For example, an apple needs little energy for storage and preparation, and the package is biodegradable. Meat and dairy products require a considerable amount of energy and resources to raise, process, deliver, keep cool at the store, keep cool at home, and then (in the case of meat) cook. So, by choosing locally produced fruits, vegetables, and grains, you can reduce your consumption of resources. Purchasing foods that are packaged for extended storage makes it possible to buy in bulk for volume discounts, saving trips to the store.

Consider Organic Foods

Today many foods are sold as organic products. An organic product is food grown without the use of pesticides or chemically formulated fertilizers.

On the label of an organic product, a more detailed list of ingredients offers a breakdown showing which ingredients are organic and which are not. Many food and consumer products with "organic" on the label are often only 70 percent or 80 percent organic. The goal is to increase the amount of organic ingredients in products. This is true with homes as well. Perhaps one day we can build an entire home from 100 percent organically grown hemp or some such material. Until then, work toward using as many organic and natural materials as possible.

Making the Most of Restaurants

With the money I'm saving from living simply, I can afford to eat out. So, if I ever want to eat a meat dish (unlikely, since I'm vegetarian), a hot dinner, or a more complete meal than I can prepare at home, I can order that kind of nutritional diversity at a restaurant. Having a fresh salad is a nice treat; however, in the past when I purchased all the ingredients for a salad, over time the ingredients would go bad before I could eat them all.

By going to a restaurant, I am purchasing the ingredients needed only for that plate of food—so there is little or no waste.

Some restaurants use Styrofoam packaging, plastic utensils, and/or do very little about food waste, so you may want to shop around for more earth-friendly places to eat.

I typically eat out every day of the week. The cost for a nice sandwich can be relatively low, and skipping the chips and fountain drink saves money, reduces fat, and reduces calories. Put some forethought into where you want to eat because not all places offer low-calorie menu items; however, you can always request changes to your meal to make it more nutritious. Don't be afraid to ask for no mayonnaise or salad dressing on the side. Sometimes these fatty items pack the most calorie punch, so by simplifying your meal, you can slim down.

Get Up and Move

Regular exercise can help you sleep more soundly at night, feel more rested on slightly less sleep, and work more effectively during the day. If you don't already have an established fitness regimen, it's important to start out small and increase your stamina over an extended period. Remember you are establishing a routine. In the beginning, don't focus entirely on how much weight you are losing, how far you are running, how many calories you are consuming, or how much weight you can lift. Instead, focus on creating a daily routine. Challenge yourself more once that routine is established. After you have a healthy regimen, the results you are looking for will happen. For example, start with a short, nonstrenuous exercise. Over time, increase the intensity and duration of the workout until you reach your goals. If you try to do too much too soon, you can injure yourself. You know that once the routine is established, if you skip a workout one day, you feel like something is missing. Maybe you experience withdrawal symptoms, almost as if you have established an addiction to that morning routine. Slowly remove those things that aren't good for you in order to maintain the healthy routine you've established.

If you have the space in your home, you may want to consider buying a piece of fitness equipment. In this way, it can easily become part of your daily routine; however, this requires an investment of money, so you may want to rent equipment first or look for used machines. A good combination of equipment would be an elliptical machine for aerobic exercise and a resistance machine for strength training.

Because fitness equipment is a considerable expense up front, you may want to join a gym for a few months to get into a fitness routine and also experiment with what equipment works best for you. If you decide that the gym is taking up too much time and you can achieve the same results at home, quit and buy the equipment to save money over time. Consider visiting a few fitness centers to use a variety of equipment before purchasing your own. Although commercial-grade equipment will be too expensive for home use, it will introduce you to a variety of machines that are available from different manufacturers. There are many brands of equipment such as NordicTrack, Pro-Form, Weider, HealthRider, Weslo, Reebok, Gold's

Gym, and others that are offered by Icon Health and Fitness based in Logan, Utah. These brands are typically available in home or commercial-grade models. If you like the commercial-grade professional model found in a fitness center, you might also like the less-expensive home version. Ultimately, your goal is better health, so your choice should be based on whatever helps you achieve that. If having a gym membership will help you stay committed, join a gym. Some people find that they just won't exercise at home because they get too distracted and there are too many interruptions. Find an exercise program that works for you and stick to it. If you get bored with one activity, such as swimming, try something different such as tennis, fencing, or salsa dancing. Keep looking until you find something that you enjoy and that keeps you healthy.

If you are genuinely pursuing a simpler life, you'll find that time and money will become available for exercise and wellness. It's essential to take advantage of this and not let your additional free time be eaten up by unproductive activities, such as watching television.

The Health of the Environment

Our personal health is closely tied to the health of the planet. For example, choosing to ride a bicycle is good for our health and produces less pollution than a car. Locally grown organic foods that are as unprocessed as possible generally require less energy to produce, store, and prepare. These foods are more nutritious and do less harm to the planet. So with this in mind, consider your personal health as well as the health of the planet while exploring simpler and smaller living.

In the human body, a signal goes from the brain to tell your muscles what to do when you want to walk. This takes a coordinated effort involving many muscles. Sometime when you are walking, put your hand in the middle of your back and feel the muscles as they do their part in moving you forward. The fact is that a single muscle working alone is not enough to allow you to walk. It takes a coordinated effort of many muscles. All it takes is for one muscle to get pulled or a ligament to get strained or sprained, and you will be slowed down to a limp. When you are at your peak of wellness, debilitating stress or strain-induced injuries are less likely.

In the same way, humanity is like a complete body. When everyone works together, great things can be accomplished. You may be the missing link (or ligament) in the body of humanity that is needed to make a difference and walk us toward a healthier future for our planet. Your example of successful, healthy living may be the motivation someone needs to take the next step.

My garbage is very minimal. Because my beverage of choice is water, I don't have pop cans, beer cans, or milk jugs that accumulate to be recycled. Most of my diet consists of fruits, vegetables, grains, and other foods that usually involve little if any packaging. When possible, I purchase bulk foods, like granola, in reusable containers. Other foods, such as carrots, bananas, melons, oranges, apples, or nuts come sealed in their own biodegradable container—the skin, peel, rind, or shell. What's left of fruits and vegetables when I'm done eating can simply be put in the garden as biodegradable compost. If all waste were this way, it could reduce the fuel used by garbage trucks. Because I live in a tiny house, I don't do a lot of excess shopping, which results in fewer packages to be thrown away. Food choices aren't always easy. Sometimes you have to decide between locally grown sources and organic sources that may be imported. Sometimes a regional provider may be doing more for the environment than your local provider. For example, if a regional provider uses all solar power and special methods of low-impact farming and your local provider doesn't, going with the regional provider may be a better choice.

The raw numbers and statistics of our global environmental challenges are difficult to grasp. Trends, such as global warming, are often presented in terms of thousands or millions of years. Environmental crises predictions or the depletion of nonrenewable resources are sometimes projected in hundreds of years. Destructive events, such as a "one-hundred-year flood," seem far off unless the last one was ninety-nine years ago.

What can a tiny human being do to impact the planet? How can the life of one individual have a positive impact, or a negative impact for that matter?

A recent exhibit by photographic artist Chris Jordan of Seattle displays a startling visual presentation of the waste created in the United States every year. On his Web site, chrisjordan.com, there are photos depicting specific items or categories of waste. When photographed, piles of discarded items, such as cell phones, circuit boards, cigarette butts, and glass bottles, create a colorful abstract ocean.

Food choices aren't always easy. Sometimes you have to decide between locally grown sources and organic sources that may be imported. Sometimes a regional provider may be doing more for the environment than your local provider.

Behind this photography project was the idea that showing people a visual image of waste might be more startling than just seeing the numbers. Yet even the visual image of the waste is hard for our minds to process. One of the pictures shows fifteen million sheets of paper, which Jordan says represents the amount of paper used in the United States every five minutes. According to Jordan, over one million plastic bags are used each day. Imagine how staggering the global statistics on waste must be.

Here are some additional figures and statistics regarding the environmental impact of consumption:

"About 94 percent of the materials extracted for use in manufacturing durable products become waste before the product is manufactured . . . [and] 80 percent of what we make is thrown away within six months of production."
—*Natural Capitalism*, Paul Hawken,
Amory Lovins, and L. Hunter Lovins

In the U.S., we generate enough trash each day to fill 44,919 garbage trucks that hold nine tons of trash each.
—"Recycling Facts and Figures,"
Wisconsin Department of Natural Resources, 2003

"Organic materials continue to be the largest component of municipal solid waste by weight: paper and paperboard products account for 35 percent of the waste stream, with yard trimmings and food scraps together accounting for about 24 percent. Plastics comprise 11 percent; metals make up 8 percent; and rubber, leather, and textiles account for about 7 percent. Wood follows at 6 percent, and glass at 5 percent. Miscellaneous wastes made up approximately 3 percent of the municipal solid waste generated in 2003."
—"Municipal Solid Waste in the United States:
2003 Facts and Figures," EPA

So, given this context, how can you—just one person—put a dent in statistics like these? How can you have an impact in the world on this and other global concerns such as poverty, health epidemics, natural disasters, war, homelessness, and starvation? Actually, you can have a greater impact than you might imagine. No matter how little you think you are doing or how unimportant you think you are, the reality is that you can't help but have a huge impact in the world because of the ripple effect. What you say and do is seen by others who will end up emulating you.

Recycle

As we begin to make recycling part of our daily routine, it becomes second nature. For recycling paper, cardboard, plastic, aluminum, glass bottles, and other items, earth911.org can help identify local recycling centers. Perhaps your community has curbside pickup of recyclable materials. The work of recycling is something we should consider as a requirement for responsible living.

Reuse and Reduce

As we become more aware of all the garbage we produce, we might begin to think of ways to reduce our overall waste, such as eating foods that come in biodegradable containers (fresh fruits and vegetables). Many grocery stores offer bulk foods, allowing us to reuse the same containers over and over. This also allows us to purchase a greater amount at one time—more suitable for our household. Storage containers can be new or leftover from some other purchase. Buying other items in bulk, such as twenty rolls of toilet paper, will require more storage either in your home or in a storage shed. As I mentioned earlier, water is an excellent alternative to carbonated beverages, alcoholic beverages, and juices because water is a product that is often available in "bulk" at the grocery store. A five-gallon container can be refilled and taken to the home or office. If you can make the shift from drinking ice water to drinking room-temperature water, then it is possible to store water without taking up space in a refrigerator.

In simplifying your life and creating space in your home, you may come up with a lot of things you want to get rid of.

Reuse bubble wrap and boxes. Use and reuse gift bags rather than use wrapping paper. Products such as Wrapsacks are a great eco-friendly alternative. Consider the environment and offer your things to family and friends, donate your belongings to a charity, donate your books to local schools and libraries, post an ad on craigslist.com, or have a garage sale. Overall reduction in our consumption is the best way to reduce our overall environmental impact.

Volunteer

Many people choose to offset their own environmental impact by giving to initiatives that help restore the environment. Volunteering is another great way to offset your own impact. The Nature Conservancy has a volunteer section on their Web site where people can join with others in their area to help restore the environment. For more information, visit nature.org/volunteer.

What Is Harmful to the Environment Is Harmful to You

If something is bad for the environment, it's safe to assume that it is harmful to humans, too. The Environmental Protection Agency offers great advice regarding safe management and disposal of waste. They recommend ways to manage and properly dispose of products in your home that could otherwise have adverse effects on your health and the health of the environment. Potentially unsafe items include the following:

- Used motor oils
- Antifreeze
- Old car batteries
- Pesticides
- Leftover paints, stains, and varnishes
- Art and photographic supplies
- Cleaning supplies

For more information, refer to the Environmental Protection Agency Web site, epa.gov/epaoswer/aging/, or check with your city to see if there are designated recycling or disposal sites for these and other potentially hazardous products.

HOW WE SIMPLIFY OUR PERSONAL HEALTH needs is directly proportional to how we can improve the environment. They go hand in hand. Make the simple, healthy choices toward improvement and see how much your life and the environment around you slim down. Remember the muscle analogy mentioned earlier in the chapter? A person cannot walk with only one muscle, and similarly, none of us can save the planet alone. Although you can make a difference in yourself and the world around you, we must be a group of muscles working in stride together.

Action Points

The following action points are ways to help better your health and the health of the environment. Select one or two to start with and slowly implement more as you simplify your life.

1. Consider having the largest portion of your diet be foods that are shelf storable, such as fresh vegetables, fresh fruit, or dried foods. This will save space and energy, since the foods need less energy for storage and preparation. Even if you can't live without a refrigerator, perhaps you can use a smaller one. Because fresh produce doesn't last long without refrigeration, buying it is only practical if there is a market close by or you eat it soon after purchase. Choose to purchase foods that are in season and locally or regionally available.

2. Have your grocery list prepared before you go shopping and buy only what's on your list. To save time, take a preprinted list of what you regularly shop for and then write down the quantities (if any) for each item. The list can be organized by grocery aisle to save you even more time while shopping and reduce impulse purchases.

3. Select one activity, such as walking, and try to integrate thirty minutes into your schedule at least three times a week. If you don't think you can do this, start with a smaller amount of time, such as fifteen minutes three times a week. That is less time than a one-hour prime-time television show.

4. Think of ways to reduce your garbage, such as eating foods that come in biodegradable containers (fresh fruits and vegetables). Take your own reusable bags with you when you go shopping.

5. Keep recyclable goods separate from trash and find a local recycling center by going to earth911.org.

Discussion Questions

Here are some discussion questions for you, your roommate(s), spouse, family, friends, or book club to consider.

1. What are two changes you can make in your eating habits for the coming week? What do you need to do to get started?

2. What exercise routine can you start with and stick to? Consider inviting a friend to exercise with you. How can you encourage yourself to reach this goal? How can you encourage someone else to reach their goal?

3. What is one change you can make right now in your daily routine to improve the health of the environment? Are you properly disposing of motor oil or cleaning supplies? Could you develop and implement a recycling plan for your home, community, or work?

Your Plan

Now it's your turn to personalize this chapter. What will you do because of what you've read?

_____

_____

_____

_____

_____

_____

_____

_____

_____

_____

_____

_____

_____

_____

_____

_____

_____

_____

_____

3

Cutting Calories from Your Livable Space

You know you have reached perfection of design not when you have nothing more to add, but when you have nothing more to take away.

—Antoine de Saint Exupèry

IT'S BEEN SAID that activism must begin at home. For those of us who are concerned about the environment and desire to have a positive impact on the world, the realm in which we have the most immediate influence is in our own home and daily living. While that may not seem as far-reaching as working with a global organization, the "think globally, act locally" approach to activism is really quite powerful, because it conveys an example that others can learn from and copy.

Starting or joining environmental initiatives in your community is a good way to broaden your impact, but you shouldn't overlook your own home.

If your first priority of activism is in simplifying your home and life, your impact in other areas can be greater since you'll likely have more time and money and you will be living what you espouse.

Although my home is only 7 x 10 feet, it doesn't feel cramped. The home was custom-built for my own needs. Since I'm about six feet tall (183 cm), the ceiling rafters are an inch or two above my head with the ceiling above those beams. This feels like just the right amount of headroom. Having windows on all four walls ensures that, in whatever direction I'm looking, my view is expansive. In fact, sitting at my desk, looking out my east window, my peripheral vision includes the 180-degree view through the north and south windows as well. It actually feels roomier than most homes. Rooms in an apartment or home typically have windows in only one or two directions, and the view and natural light (a natural mood enhancer) are usually limited, increasing the demand for electricity for artificial lighting.

You may be thinking: *How could I ever live in a house the size of yours? I feel crowded in the house I'm already in. There's no way!* You may never live in a house the size of mine, but I promise you that you can simplify your life enough to be happier, less stressed out, and more conscious of the things you buy. With homes, there's no such thing as one size fits all, and it is difficult to settle on an ideal square-feet-per-person formula. Much of what determines the right size for the inside of your home will be how you utilize the space available to you. If you have a fitness center, laundry, and health food store within a few blocks, then your kitchen can be smaller, you won't need room for fitness equipment, and it's not a problem if you don't have a washer and dryer. Something I've done for many years, even before moving into a small home, is to define an area as my "living space" that can be free of clutter. Things I don't need on a daily or weekly basis get stored in a basement, garage, or storage facility. This allows me to have the immediate benefit of simple and organized living in the space where I spend the most time.

For many people, the size of a home doesn't matter as much as its location or simply how the space "feels" when you first see it. A couple or family might live in a home that feels just right for them, even if it's a bit small. They agree that they'll make it work, and they do make it work. Throughout the rest of the chapter we will be discussing ways to simplify your space so that it can "work" for you.

Evaluate Your Space

Perhaps it's not that your home is too small, but that you aren't using your space creatively. Rooms reflect areas of life such as sleeping (bedroom), eating (kitchen/dining room), personal hygiene (bathroom), exercising (fitness room), and socializing (living room). When these areas of our home overflow into another room, it's an indication that our life may be getting out of balance. The first step is to consider one room at a time. Just as you have defined your personal priorities, consider the purpose of each room in your home (i.e., for entertainment, for privacy, etc.) and then make sure everything in the room serves that purpose. You are not only analyzing used space but also potentially wasted space. This exercise can help you evaluate how balanced your life is.

- Is everything in the bedroom conducive to sleep?
- Is the living room an enjoyable place to entertain or is it filled with clutter?
- Is your bathroom overrun with an excessive number of products?

Until you are able to part with excess clutter, consider storing it somewhere. When taking a look at your home, consider how every little inch can be used efficiently. My bedroom is in the loft area (or attic) of my house, where the peak of the roof is. In most homes, this area is either unfinished or wasted space. As you think about each room in your home, including your garage, I guarantee you will identify wasted space.

- Is there a spot underneath your stairs that you've been using to store junk that could be turned into a child's playroom or a private nook?
- What could you do with a room that is currently filled with boxes or bins of unused items?
- When was the last time you cleaned out your home storage room or storage unit—actually opening up boxes with the purpose of getting rid of stuff?
- Are there places in your home or storage room where you could install shelves to organize boxes or seasonal items?

Consider what you will need to do to ensure that the purpose of a room matches what you envision it to be. If you're just storing boxes, the room doesn't need to have permanent lighting or finished floors, walls, or ceiling. Storage areas can be built at a much lower cost per square foot than livable areas. If you are using a finished, livable room as a storage room, it may be wasted space. Be bold in examining your home. I promise there is more room there than you think.

Making Your Home Feel Larger

None of us like the feeling of life closing in on us. When our schedules are busy, our finances are tight, and our homes are filled with clutter, we may feel that the scarcity of time and money is constricting the space around us. Claustrophobia is not always a result of being in a physically small space—you may be living alone in a 3,000 square-foot home and still feel claustrophobic. The contentment you feel with your surroundings is created by what's projected from inside you, not the other way around. The goal is to simplify your space until you find contentment within yourself and your home.

Floor Plan. A problem with some larger homes and apartments is that they aren't designed efficiently. This is why some homes that are three or four times the size of mine can still feel cramped. A home that is designed from the ground up can be better designed to utilize a smaller space more efficiently. If you aren't able to build a small home, make the best use of the space you have. For example, customized shelving and storage can be built in to use every inch of space efficiently, rather than adding furniture that sort-of fits. You can also try switching the function of your rooms. Perhaps your spare storage room could be changed to a hobby room.

Color. The colors we choose for carpet, paint, fixtures, and other elements in our home are a very personal decision. One thing to keep in mind is that lighter colors and smooth reflective surfaces can help disperse lighting, making a room feel more spacious. In some cases, natural lighting is sufficient to brighten a room during the day, but if heavy drapes or blinds cover the windows and there are dark colors in a room, the space may not look or feel bright even with artificial lighting.

Furniture and Décor. One of the largest consumers of our space is the furniture we choose and how we decorate a room. Furniture and décor are often purchased because they "fit" in the current space we are in. Then we move them to the next home without regard to the space they are moving into. Consider using furniture that stores easily, such as folding chairs, folding tables, or a futon couch that can fold out into a bed for guests.A properly designed slimmed-down home will have an interior that is proportionately consistent so that to the eye everything is the same relative size to that which is in a larger home. For example, the sink in my home is significantly smaller than an average-size sink, but its dimensions are to scale so it doesn't look small.

I have a collection of tiny books. This helps reinforce the smaller scale of the home.

By having common household objects that are smaller scale, the mind interprets the surroundings as being of normal dimensions. The rules for efficient use of space are fairly consistent and apply to small, medium, and large homes.

If there's a room in your home with furniture or décor that doesn't get used or is not proportional to the space, consider redesigning the function of that room or moving the objects to another part of your home where they might be better utilized.

The best option is to make use of what you have, but another option is to purchase new furniture and décor when you move into a new apartment or home. This way you can buy just what you need and not simply be storing unused furniture and miscellaneous items that do not mesh with your new home.

Other Things to Consider

If you are already feeling cramped in the home you are in, windows, art, mirrors, textures, colors, and plenty of light are essential elements in letting smaller spaces feel larger. Also consider the following:

- Music can help create a sense of expanded space around you. In fact, the acoustics of music can "trick" your mind into making you feel that you are in a big hall or at a live concert.
- Watching a movie or television on your computer with a pair of headphones can take you to another space.
- Taking time out to meditate on what's inside of you and the vastness of the universe that surrounds you can help expand your view beyond the immediate surroundings.
- Remind yourself that your home expands beyond four walls to include the local park, shopping areas, and restaurants.

Eliminate the Unnecessary

You don't have to throw everything out to simplify your life; you just have to be smart about what you keep and what you give away. The challenging part about downsizing doesn't have anything to do with getting rid of things. What's really hard about the process is to first determine what your priorities are regarding your possessions. It can be difficult to decide what to keep and what to throw away if you haven't clearly defined what the object is for. When you do the evaluation of your space, it should help you realize that everything you have should serve a purpose. Once you know the purpose of your possessions, deciding what to eliminate will be easier.

One suggestion that may help is to look at how people lived a hundred years ago. In the "old days," people weren't collectors of unnecessary items—it wasn't practical or affordable. The blacksmith would have some clothes and simple belongings for daily living and the tools of his trade. The same was true for the shoemaker, the baker, and the candlestick maker. They would decide what their calling was in life, and then they could own the tools needed just for that line of work. This may be an approach you would like to take. Keep only the "stuff" pertinent to your vocation.

Make Friends with the Storage Facility

People have asked me, "Was it hard to sort out what was important enough to keep in your home?" The greatest help to me on the journey toward minimalism was the use of a storage facility. I would have had a difficult time parting with my possessions; however, distancing myself from them was something I could do. The benefits were immediate.

I didn't want to spend a lot of time laboring over what to keep in my home and what to put into storage, so I decided to put everything in storage. I only kept the few things I would need on a daily basis, the kinds of things I might take on a vacation. Putting my possessions into storage wasn't the same as selling them rashly or giving them away on impulse, because I could always retrieve anything I might want. It made the decision process easier. After years of not using or even thinking about something, I realized that I had never really needed it at all. I simply enjoyed owning stuff, and some objects had purely sentimental value. I realized I could take photos of some mementos and keepsakes instead of keeping them, and it preserved the memory of an item that would have ended up in storage for years anyway. Slowly the unused objects of my life became simpler to part with.

> For me, it was very liberating to split my life into two spaces: storage and living.

Increasingly, my living space became more minimalist and tranquil.

You can take this one step further and apply it to your office space. Trim down your office to what is really practical. Don't save every professional journal. Scan articles of interest or subscribe to email or online alternatives. Don't stock up on every extra tool and part. Focus on only what is useful on a regular basis. And if you

Outsourcing is the same principle as delegating work, but it is also delegating the ownership and care of things or facilities to other people.

happen to change your career or go back to school in a different field, box up your old materials and keep them in storage until you know for sure that you no longer need them.

By putting your possessions in storage, you will know after a year or two of nonuse which items were really important and which ones were not. This takes much of the thinking and guesswork out of the process. Collecting and hoarding are common but irrational behaviors. You may go back to your storage facility a year or two later and find that you still don't want to get rid of anything. Rationally you know that many of those things are not necessary, yet it can still be hard to part with them. It's okay. You can wait a little longer and see how it goes, but remember that you are paying rent for items that you may not ever need or use. What is the replacement cost of those items? For the hundreds of dollars you are spending on rental fees, could that money be used to eventually purchase the "I might need that someday" items when you actually need them?

Consider Outsourcing

A smaller or simpler house can be designed to meet the needs of its inhabitant(s) and also have an effective symbiotic relationship with its surroundings. The term "outsourcing" has come to have somewhat negative connotations for many people; yet outsourcing one's life on a micro scale can be very empowering. Outsourcing is the same principle as delegating work, but it is also delegating the ownership and care of things or facilities to other people. For example, when you go out to a restaurant, you are outsourcing the work for creating the meals you purchase—going grocery shopping, cooking the meal, and doing the dishes. Whether one looks at it as giving up ownership of things or giving over responsibility of tasks, the end result is the same.

When I lived in a 2,000-square-foot home, doing yard work, shoveling snow, and performing regular maintenance and upkeep of the home and property became like a part-time job. When I moved into a tiny home, I replaced that part-time job with a paying part-time job—consulting. Spending even just ten hours per month on maintaining my home, which time is now spent consulting, added up to thousands of opportunity dollars lost per year. For some of you, yard work or cooking is a wonderful hobby. Keep what's important to you and what makes you happy, and eliminate other things that aren't so important and take up your time.

Think about items in your house you enjoy that could just as easily be in a shared community clubhouse:

- piano
- fireplace
- patio
- big yard
- garden
- tennis courts

- swimming pool
- hot tub
- putting green
- exercise room
- pool table

- ping-pong table
- library
- atrium

Although my life has become smaller and simpler, I'm still living in about 2,000 square feet when I consider all of the spaces I outsource on a regular day. It's just that I'm only responsible for the upkeep of 140 square feet out of the 2,000. Outsourcing can also be a great way to be a part of society and meet new people. When you outsource those items in your home that are currently a source of wasted space, you are simplifying your life and reducing the amount of time, money, and energy you spend on that space.

Make Your Space Multifunctional

When you evaluate your space, think how you can make your rooms more multifunctional. For example, perhaps you're contemplating or have already started a home-based business to generate some extra income and enjoy some tax benefits. Rather than building on a new office, you can downsize your own needs within your existing home.

Perhaps a corner of your family room can double as your office. In this way, a room that was not previously a profit center can generate cash flow and a tax break.

Evaluating your space and then doing a little research about home-based businesses is all it takes to get started. If you consider that a profit-generating office is simply a room with electricity and a window, it doesn't matter whether it is in a high-rise office building or a small room in your basement.

My home "office" is a 7 x 10-foot room that consists of a small desk area where I put my notebook computer and some storage cabinets. It's a wonderful space to work, framed in by bookshelves on both sides and a window in front of me. When I'm working, I only use about 3 x 4 feet. When I'm not working, the whole room becomes my kitchen and dining area. Since I live in a one-room house, that one room needs to serve multiple functions. For homes with multiple rooms, the "office" often has a bed in it, allowing the room to serve as a guest room. The principle is the same. Even a family room can take up less space now that flat screen televisions and smaller home video components are available. Comfortable folding chairs or easily stored furniture can allow a room to grow and shrink based on the current need.

Living small doesn't mean people can't come and visit you.

Don't let space keep you from inviting people over.

There's more of it than you might imagine. In fact, regardless of the size of your home, if it is less cluttered and easier to keep clean, you'll be more likely to invite friends over. Socializing in larger venues, like sports arenas, large reception centers, or dance halls, can make it hard to have a quiet and meaningful conversation. Socializing in a smaller setting can be more personal. Having furniture that easily folds and stores is a nice way to make room for guests.

Keeping Your Spaces Slimmed Down: How to Avoid Recluttering

Once you have gained control of your space, here are some tips to avoid clutter and to not run into the same problems all over again:

- Shop and drop. The shop-and-drop principle is that for everything you buy—every pair of shoes, every appliance, every book—you get rid of one or more items that are less necessary. In this way, your material possessions either stay at the same level or decrease over time.
- Buy small. As you buy replacement items, purchase the smaller version of appliances, electronics, furniture, and other such things.
- Set boundaries. Having a place for everything and everything in its place can be a great way of setting boundaries. If you don't have room for more cookware or dishes, don't buy them. Only buy what you have space for.

NO MATTER HOW YOU CHOOSE TO SLIM DOWN your livable space, you can make it work for you. Evaluating your home for useable areas and down-sizing your possessions can be difficult at first, but if you start small, I guarantee that you can make a difference in your home and begin the process of simplifying your life. Creating a simpler and smaller living space is a freeing experience.

Action Points

The following action points are some ways to streamline your space and keep it slimmed down. Select one or two to start with and slowly implement more as you simplify your life.

1. Take everything out of the bathroom except the bare essentials. What would you take on a very short relaxing and casual weekend trip? Can you live with that at home? Try it out to see for yourself.

2. Select one main living area and evaluate how much of the space is used and how much is wasted. Develop a plan to slim down your space and then implement your plan. Write down how well it went and what you learned.

3. Make your space multifunctional. What areas of your home could serve dual purposes?

4. Find three practical things you could outsource in your home and choose one to implement for a week. Evaluate how it goes and if you could outsource even more to create space in your home. If it works for you, consider how much money and time you could save by moving into a simpler and smaller space.

5. Set boundaries and have a place for everything you own. Start with your bedroom closet. Make two piles: (1) belongings you've used in the last six months and (2) belongings you haven't touched in the last six months. Put all items you can't part with from pile number two in a box labeled "Closet Excess" or decide where they should go so that you start using them. Write the date on the box and keep it in your storage unit for a year. When a year has passed and you don't remember what's in the box, donate it to a local charity.

Discussion Questions

Here are some discussion questions for you, your roommate(s), spouse, family, friends, or book club to consider.

1. Look around your home for wasted space. Do you have items in your home that can go into an unfinished storage room rather than taking up space in a finished area? Is it worth the money to you to rent a storage unit to free up space in your home? Brainstorm with your friends and loved ones to come up with ideas for their homes as well as your own.

2. Simplify. Reducing your possessions and commitments of time and money can help make you much more focused, effective, and peaceful. What are your priorities for each room? Discuss this with friends or family, and once you've decided, follow through to make that space fit what you envisioned.

Your Plan

Now it's your turn to personalize this chapter. What will you do because of what you've read?

_____

_____

_____

_____

_____

_____

_____

_____

_____

_____

_____

_____

_____

_____

_____

_____

_____

_____

_____

4

How Green Is Your Home?

Reduce the complexity of life by
eliminating the needless wants
of life, and the labors of life
reduce themselves.

—Edwin Way Teale

I CHOSE TO HAVE my home built without a shower, toilet, and full kitchen for various reasons. I very much wanted my home to be off the water, sewer, and electric grid. A home that is freestanding without electricity or plumbing is much less expensive to build, and it isn't impacted by electrical and sewer installation building codes. Even in the best of homes, pipes can leak or freeze, causing costly damage. Toilets can back up and overflow, and septic systems are costly to build, maintain, and repair. Municipal water service results in a monthly water bill. These are all extra unnecessary expenses and hassles. At home, I eat mostly natural and organic foods that require no energy in their preparation to eat, so for the past three years I've rarely had to wash dishes in my home. This has saved a considerable amount of water.

My lifestyle may seem extreme, but it suits me very well. I have figured out how to save money while reducing my carbon footprint. Even if I were to move back into a larger home, I would still be making lifestyle choices to cut my bills and be more environmentally conscious—the principle of living small and simply is the same regardless of the size of your home.

The amount of money a person saves by living "small" depends on how much they were spending when they were living "big."

In my case, the 2,000-square-foot home I lived in previously cost about $1,000 per month, including all housing expenses. Since my house is now physically smaller and I have taken measures to be economical with how I use energy and water, I spend very little money on utilities. In housing and utilities alone, I save around $10,000 a year. By living in a community supportive of walking and biking, I was able to sell my car and save another several thousand dollars per year. Knowing how much money you will save by living simply will help you make decisions about your current home and any future homes. You can figure out what size house works best for you and choose one that will save you money and also have the least impact on the environment.

Utilities

For most people, utility costs are a significant portion of their monthly housing expense. Without having to completely do away with these bills, there are significant things you can do to lower your water, electric, and gas bills.

Water Doesn't Grow on Trees, But Trees Grow on Water

Given that water is now an extremely expensive liquid and that billions of people don't have access to clean water, we should be more mindful about the water we use. Imagine having a water bill that is $72 . . . per day! At a cost of $36 per .75L bottle, some higher-priced waters could cost more than $2,000 per month—and that's just for drinking water (assuming 1.5L per day). Of course, less expensive waters are available for as little as about $1.50 per .5L bottle, costing a mere $135 a month (again assuming you drink about 1.5L per day).

Years ago, the cost of bottled water exceeded that of gasoline. In September 2005, Garry Emmons wrote a little-known article titled "Water Ltd." that appeared in the Harvard alumni bulletin. The following month, in October 2005, the Harvard Business School publication *Working Knowledge* featured an article by Emmons titled "Turning on the Tap: Is Water the Next Oil?" which expanded on his original writing about the global demand for clean water. Today, wars are being fought over oil wells, but some predict that future wars may be fought over water wells. At present, over one billion people do not have access to clean water and over two billion people do not have access to sanitation systems. In parts of the world where fresh water is abundant, it is often wasted. In the United States, some areas have a rich supply of water, yet other areas experience shortages and have water rationing. Because water is a constant on our planet, and the population is still growing in many countries, the number of people without access to water is increasing. What can you do to help the situation? Let me tell you what I do.

I like to purchase filtered tap water from the grocery store at about 25 cents per gallon—much less expensive than the $36 per .75L bottle I mentioned above. I typically refill several five-gallon containers at the store to last me a few weeks, so my "water bill" for the drinking water is under $5 per month. Counter-top water filtration systems are an inexpensive option for people who would like filtered water at home for a cost of pennies per gallon. The water I use on a daily basis to shower, wash my hands, brush my teeth, and do dishes is provided without any additional charge—either at the gym or at my place of employment. The little bit of water I use at home is mostly for brushing my teeth at night. I usually go through about two gallons per week and can refill those containers as needed with tap water.

I've noticed that carrying my water home makes me more conscientious of how much water I use.

Giving up running water in the home is an extreme choice, and depending on where you live, the cost of gym membership isn't necessarily less than a monthly water bill. So, choosing to be off the water grid is simply for those who want the experience and would be paying for a gym membership anyway. You'll be limited to the hours and days that the gym is open.

We can all benefit from conserving water. How much water do you think you use a day? You may be surprised how quickly those gallons add up, especially when you start to calculate how many times you flush the toilet, rinse a dish off, and wash your hands. All of us can be a little more water conscious, so here are some ideas that have been proven most beneficial:

➤ Cooking. The cookware and dishes you use to prepare and eat greasy and processed foods are often those that require the most water to get clean. You can eat healthier foods, such as organic fresh fruit, vegetables, and dried foods with few, if any, utensils, cookware, and dishes. This reduces water required for cleaning up after a meal. When doing dishes, use a smaller container as your dishpan and then rinse dishes in clean or sanitized standing water rather than under running water (this is what the pros do).

- Dishwasher. Hand-washing dishes twice a day uses about eighteen gallons of water. Running a dishwasher uses about eleven gallons. Never run a dishwasher that's only half full.
- Faucets. Fix leaks. Get low-flow fixtures.
- Hoses and sprinklers. Put a nozzle on the end of your garden hose so the water isn't always running. Water your lawn and garden in the early hours of the morning.
- Lawn care. Incorporate permaculture (permanent agriculture) into your landscaping. Trees, shrubs, and plants that are natural to your environment will be lower maintenance and thrive on natural precipitation. This can save huge amounts of water. If you live in a desert, don't try to maintain a yard full of lush green grass that needs hundreds of gallons of water to stay alive. Using regionally appropriate plants can save you time and money.
- Running water. When brushing your teeth, don't leave the water running. Instead, wet the brush before and rinse the brush afterward. When shaving, fill up the sink with water and rinse your razor off as needed. Don't forget to turn off the water while washing your hands.
- Shower. It's easy to daydream and lose track of time while in the shower. For many people, the shower is a moment during the day to relax and zone out. For relaxation, consider an alternative to showering. To cut back on your time in the shower, put a countdown timer near the shower. If you're used to taking fifteen-minute showers, start by setting the countdown timer alarm for twelve minutes. Then work down to ten minutes and so on. Turn the water off when you're lathering up.
- Toilet. A leaky toilet can lose over forty thousand gallons of water per year. Fixing leaks is inexpensive and saves money. When leaky toilets clog they can overflow, resulting in thousands of dollars in damage. It's certainly possible to have a bathroom and shower in a small home. These amenities can be identical to those in a standard residence. Newer technologies for toilets are available that don't require water or plumbing. If you use a tiny moveable home for vacations and camping, then it may be equipped with the same type of showers and restroom facilities that are used in campers and RVs.

- Washing machine. It takes forty to sixty gallons of water to wash one load of clothes. That's about 20 percent of indoor water use. Be aware that you can wash your clothes at a laundromat to save space in your home and spend less money on an electric bill, but you're still using the same amount of water. Always wash large loads. Plan ahead so that you don't do a small load just because you need something that instant. Or wash socks and undergarments daily in a small amount of water, letting them dry overnight.
- Technology. Numerous water-saving devices are now economically available, including low-flow toilets, showerheads, and faucets.

Visit the Web site wateruseitwisely.com for one hundred suggestions on how to reduce your water usage. Because many of the practices above require behavioral changes, you may need to do just a few each week and incorporate them into your new habits of living.

Water calculators are a great way to get you thinking about your water usage. Go to fowd.com/images/WaterUseCalculator.swf for one example.

Electricity Simplicity

I first began using an electricity usage worksheet when considering the purchase of a backup electric generator for the larger home I was living in many years ago. An electricity worksheet is simply a piece of paper listing all of your household appliances with their wattage. You can create one by hand or type one on a computer. The wattage of appliances is usually written somewhere on its label. Electric generators are rated based on their wattage of output. So, in purchasing a generator, I needed to determine how many watts of continuous power I might need. It was then that I realized that owning lower-power appliances really reduces the cost of a generator, since lower-wattage generators cost less to purchase and operate. For about $30 or less, devices like the Kill-A-Watt Electricity Usage Monitory by P3 International help evaluate how much electricity an appliance consumes in a day. Such devices can also be used to measure multiple appliances using the same power strip. Online calculators like generator sales.com/calculator_google.asp can help determine how much power a household is using.

Later I used an electricity worksheet to determine what kind of investment I would need to make in solar, wind, and battery storage to get off the grid. I realized how power hungry my inefficient appliances were.

I used an electricity worksheet to determine what kind of investment I would need to make in solar, wind, and battery storage to get off the grid. I realized how power hungry my inefficient appliances were.

It's costly to take a home that was designed for regular power usage and put it on solar power. It's like taking a Hummer and then trying to retrofit it for a small electric motor. Homes designed for low-power usage work better with solar and alternative power.

However, here are some suggestions that can work in any size home:

- Air conditioning and heating. Consider using a small high-efficiency air conditioner in the main rooms of your house. In the wintertime, use a small high-efficiency heater. At night, turn the thermostat down to 58 degrees and bundle up under the covers.

- Appliances. Unplug appliances that aren't in use. Many appliances still drain electricity even when they are off. Go with low-power appliances and camping gear when possible. Many of these devices work just as well as their power-hungry counterparts.

- Clothes dryer. Wear lightweight clothes and let the high-speed spin cycle on a front-loading washer get your clothes almost dry—this cuts your drying time in half. Then line-dry your clothes to get them completely dry.

- Computer. Notebook computers are typically the least power intensive of computers. Whatever computer you use, make sure you utilize all available power-saving features. Put the computer into sleep mode when you are away from it for short periods of time or power it entirely off for longer periods of time. Apple offers this helpful online calculator that can show cost savings over time: apple.com /environment/resources/calculator.html.

- Cooking. Use an outside barbeque in the summer instead of the kitchen stove to avoid heating up the house. When you use the kitchen, keep it enclosed and ventilated with a fan so that the heat from the kitchen will not get into the rest of the house.

- Entertainment. If you've made the transition to a notebook computer, you can save a considerable amount of energy by listening to your music and viewing movies on your computer, as well as listening to the radio and watching television online. For the kids, consider board games, trucks, dolls, and other toys that don't require electricity but instead are fueled by the children's imagination.

- Light. LED lighting is the latest technology to provide amazingly bright light on very little energy. Most LED lighting systems offer bulbs that never need replacing. They can be run on rechargeable batteries or plugged into the wall. Fluorescent lights are also an option. They use 75 percent less energy and last ten times longer than an incandescent bulb. If you're going to be out of a room or not using the light for more than five minutes, turn it off.

Lightweight clothing

Lightweight clothes can be washed with less soap and water, and dried in half the time. For example, the outfitter ExOfficio sells travel pants that look like dress pants, except they are much lighter and can be washed by hand and dried on the line in a hotel room. They are very comfortable. Lightweight clothes have less fabric to absorb perspiration and body odor, so you can wash them less frequently than heavier clothing. By layering in the wintertime, you can have all-season clothing. This saves closet space. If you wash your clothes at a laundry facility, you'll end up spending less on washing, drying, and detergent. If you wash at home and plan to eventually replace your washer and dryer, you can consider smaller appliances that are more energy efficient. Using a clothesline for drying is also more practical for those who wear lightweight clothes.

Most of the year I don't need electricity in my home; however, in the summer, I recharge a twelve-volt deep-cycle battery to provide power for two fans to cool the house. Recharging the battery doesn't take long, and I can typically plug it in just about anywhere. The fans draw .32 amps each, and the battery has a 105-amp-per-hour capacity. Once fully charged, the battery can provide over 330 hours of use for one fan or 165 hours of use for two fans. This is sufficient for two to four weeks, assuming the fans are going eight hours per day. The amount of electricity I use at home over a two-month period is less than most homes require in a single day. If I ever need to, I can use an inverter connected to my deep-cycle batteries to create regular household AC current. My home is wired with outlets for this purpose. For much of the summer, I cool the house at night by leaving the windows open, and then I close them up during the day to retain the cool night air. This can result in the daytime indoor temperature being ten to twenty degrees cooler than the outside temperature.

In the summer, a simple indoor/outdoor thermometer is an excellent tool to quickly identify if the outdoor temperature has dropped below the indoor temperature, signaling that it is time to open the windows. During a warm but comfortable summer day, there are plenty of cross breezes in a house that has windows on every wall. You can open and close windows in various directions depending on the direction the wind is blowing. As with sailing a boat, you quickly become attentive to the direction of the wind to harness its power.

Gas On, Gas Off

In some regions, gas appliances are less expensive than their electric-powered equivalent. Typical gas appliances include stoves, hot water heaters, and heating systems. Here are some suggestions for cutting back on your gas bill:

▸ Furnace filter. Change your furnace filters regularly and save a lot of money, in addition to keeping your home free of dust.

▸ Heater. Depending on your home and living situation, alternatives to heating may be available that require very little electricity and do not use traditional fuels. Biomass radiant heating systems use pellets that consist of biodegradable nontoxic materials that are locally available such as sawdust, corn, or other inexpensive industry by-products. As with any heating system, the cost of use depends on where you live (what fuels are locally available), how well insulated your home is, and how long and cold your winters are. In general, the biomass-fueled heating systems cost less to purchase and operate than electric or gas systems. Some of the biomass heating systems will adapt to a variety of fuels, allowing you to choose the least expensive fuel in any given year.

▸ Home insulation. Consider going through your home one room at a time and determining how best to weatherproof each room. Insulation is relatively inexpensive, considering the benefit and payback from it. Be sure to have as much insulation in the attic as possible. Weather stripping outside is also helpful. Special temperature-sensitive video or photography can help determine where your house is leaking. The cost to have someone survey your home is generally inexpensive and will help you determine where to start plugging leaks. As an alternative to paying a professional, you can go to an auto parts store and, for about $70, purchase a laser thermometer to measure surface temperatures. These futuristic devices will tell you the surface temperature of a wall or object from across the room with laser pinpoint accuracy. Start by measuring around windows, wall switches, and outlets. These are areas typically susceptible to heat loss (or gain in the summer).

- Shower. Water heaters take gas, oil, or electricity to heat the water, so if you take long showers, you are not only wasting water but also other resources. Take showers, not baths, and find an efficient showerhead. An on-demand water heater might also be a practical solution.

- Stove. For many areas of the country, a gas stove will cost less to use than electric. In either case, consider mixing foods into your diet that don't require lots of time on the stove. Since high heat generally depletes the nutritional value of veggies and other foods, cooking less can save time, save money, and be better for you.

- Washing machine. Up to 90 percent of the energy used for washing clothes goes to heat the water, so always wash clothes in cold water. It will not only save you money, but your clothes will also last longer.

The cost of LP (liquefied petroleum, or propane) gas for heating during the cold Iowa winters is not very high. The benefit of using LP gas is that twenty pound containers are easily refilled at many retailers, and they are small enough to transport easily. Because my house is small and heavily insulated, it takes very little to heat the house and keep it warm. The heater in the house is designed for a small cabin in a boat, so it works very well for my nearly airtight home. The heater brings fresh air from outside into the combustion chamber and then exhausts the hot air back outside so that no oxygen from inside is burned up in the process. The airflow is automatic because the hot air rises. The heater can operate without electricity, unlike most home heating systems where if the electricity fails the heating does too—which can be life threatening in severe climates. In recent years, thousands of people in the United States have gone days or weeks without heat during severe winter cold because of electricity outages.

The fuel tanks for my home are the same as those used on an outdoor gas grill for cooking. They cost about $16 to refill where I live in Iowa, but prices vary around the country. Some months a single container is all I use. In the cooler months of the year, when the nighttime temperature is above freezing but still cold, I open up the windows in the daytime to let in the warmer daytime air. Then I close the windows at night when the outside temperature drops below a comfortable range. Because the house is so well insulated, it maintains the comfortable temperature all night, enhanced by body heat. It's easier to control airflow in the summer and winter in a smaller home, and it's only during the severely cold or hot months that artificially assisted climate control is necessary.

Create a Main Living Area

Each person has varying degrees of conservation in mind when using water, electricity, heat, and air conditioning, so your results may vary. If you are currently in a large home (or need to move into a large home) and want to keep utility costs as low as possible, consider making a tiny "home" inside just one room of the larger home. Here are some examples of how you might do this.

- Make one room in your home the primary living space for working, eating, and sleeping. Heat and cool only that portion of the home on a regular basis. By using smaller spot cooling and heating systems you can cut down on costs. Purchase a small microwave and small refrigerator to create a kitchenette for that room.
- If necessary, remove existing windows (only in that room of the house) and replace them with the most expensive high-efficiency windows. This can further help make that room the most energy-efficient one in the house. During severe heat or cold, maintaining a comfortable temperature in that one room (rather than the entire house) can save energy.
- If you are considering a move to a smaller home and are trying to find out how much space might be comfortable, begin by downsizing within your existing home or apartment so that when you do make the move, the transition isn't so challenging.

How Big Is Too Big?
Finding the Home that Fits

For some people, choosing the right-size home may be determined by their financial budget rather than the amount of space they desire. Mortgage payments, utility bills, and ongoing maintenance costs can be significantly different depending on the size of a home. It's important to calculate all the anticipated costs of maintaining a home. Include expected and unexpected expenses. For example, include the cost of replacing the furnace in a reasonable period of time. Don't think, "Well, we'll figure out how we can afford that when it happens." Plan ahead for those things. Consider buying way below what you think you can afford to create a financial buffer for yourself. Purchasing a home that is well within your budget could allow you to make larger payments and pay it off sooner, saving thousands of dollars in interest fees. Because a house payment or rent is one of the largest expenses we have, eliminating it as soon as possible is essential. In general, a smaller home has less that can break down and requires less energy to heat and cool (all other factors being equal). There are many modifications a person can make to an existing home to make it more energy efficient; yet a home that's been built with energy efficiency in mind from the very beginning will generally be less expensive over time.

Building Your Small Home

If you are in a position to build a small home, the rewards are significant. In building smaller, it is economically feasible to purchase the best-quality materials since fewer materials are needed in construction. If you are planning to purchase an existing home, look for a home that was constructed with energy efficiency in mind, or at least a house that can be retrofitted and redesigned to be highly efficient. Reducing the size of the home will reduce the cost of ownership, so consider all of the available methods for better utilizing space. By using one room for several functions, a home with fewer rooms may work for you. By downsizing before making a move or home purchase, you can avoid thinking you need more space than you really do and save all around. It's like eating before going grocery shopping to keep from buying food purely based on your hunger pains. Downsize your needs before looking for a home. The cost to build my home was about $15,000, including labor payments at a discounted rate. Since I contributed to the construction of the home, the cost was also dramatically reduced. To have a home like mine built today would

Purchasing a home that is well within your budget could allow you to make larger payments and pay it off sooner, saving thousands of dollars in interest fees.

probably cost about $30,000. Other homes of similar size could be built for substantially less money; however, the materials would not be as good as those used in my home. There is a perception that small homes are of poorer quality than larger homes. In reality, many larger homes are built with poor-quality materials, because high-quality materials would simply make the house too expensive. By choosing to build a smaller home, you are freer to use higher-quality materials since the overall cost of construction won't be excessive and because the result will be lower maintenance cost and lower utility bills over time. It is also realistic to use more time-consuming building techniques that result in a sturdier and longer-lasting home that needs less maintenance. Low- and zero-maintenance construction options, which are initially more expensive, will save money and natural resources in the long run.

This is similar to the auto industry, where higher-quality cars are available for slightly more money at the time of purchase but in the long run may have a lower cost of ownership and will hold their value longer. Often people fall into the trap of purchasing something that's inexpensive because that's all they can afford. They don't realize that they are perpetuating a poverty condition in their life by always purchasing the cheapest thing that ultimately costs more to own over its lifetime in replacement and upkeep costs.

If the law would permit it, I'd like to build a one-story, 12 x 16-foot cottage of stone or wood with a slab foundation and a fireplace. I'd want the house to look very quirky—like something out of a storybook fairytale.

I would like to build a village of tiny cottages that shared the same community center.

I think this would be the ideal way to live, because each person could enjoy the privacy and independence of home ownership while at the same time having the economic benefits of sharing facilities like a kitchen, bathroom, shower, laundry, and fitness facilities. Today it is common for such resources to be multiplied out into millions of households, resulting in unnecessary expense.

Land

People often ask me about land and home construction issues. Although there are some similarities, land and building requirements are different all over the country. In many areas, the law requires that homes be at least 1,200 square feet, for example, while in other areas of the country, people are free to build with any materials they like and any size they like. It's important to thoroughly investigate all the restrictions in an area before purchasing land for building. Laws regarding home construction may vary considerably from one county to the next even within the same state.

Having a Green-Friendly Home

There are two ways to consider how environmentally friendly a home is. Most simply, an environmentally friendly home is one that is designed to use very little energy for lighting and heat. In this sense, my home is very efficient and, therefore, environmentally friendly. An additional consideration when building an environmentally friendly home concerns what the building materials are made of. Are they safe? For example, a material may be an excellent insulator (saving energy), yet it could also emit toxic fumes. What resources were used and what pollution was generated in the production of the building materials? Another consideration is the waste generated at the building site. Can the packaging, by-products, and extra materials be recycled? Are any of the materials toxic? A home that is very energy efficient and "green" may not be the best from an environmental standpoint if it uses materials that negatively impacted the environment in their creation and will negatively affect the earth with long-term use.

Most of the materials used in the construction of my home were glass, solid natural wood, or metal.

The siding is solid cedar wood, and the interior of the house is made with solid pine. I chose not to use paint, wallpaper, or other finishing materials. Instead, the interior walls, ceiling, cabinets, and shelves were left untreated except for the floor surfaces, which were protected against water damage or scratching. The kitchen and desk surfaces are stainless steel. So, in this regard, my home and its materials are safe to use and easy on the environment. The solid pink-board insulation is one of the nonorganic materials used. Extra insulation adds to the cost of building a home; however, it pays for itself in the long run. And, ideally, we should use local materials for the construction of our homes. My hope is that the energy savings from having high-efficiency insulation will offset the environmental impact of its creation.

An important part of having a green home (house or apartment) is to consider its location in proximity to your work and where you will be spending most of your time. A home that is "green" for one person may not be "green" for another, simply because the one person may need to drive two hours round-trip every day to work. Consider the "greenness" of your home or apartment from a holistic perspective.

Things to Consider for a Green Home

Before investing in high-efficiency windows, insulation, low-power lighting, water-saving appliances, and other energy-saving products, most of us would like to be sure that these devices will save us money over time and that the savings will exceed the cost of installation. Because each home is unique and every region of the country has its own climate, it is difficult to provide generalized statements about how much money you will save or what percentage reduction in your utility bill you can expect. Purchase costs may vary from one brand to the next—will you be buying the items on sale? Labor costs may be significant—will you install the products yourself? Use the following chart as a general guide.

- Use alternative forms of lighting, such as LED lighting or compact fluorescent lights.
- Solar power could provide the electricity needed for lighting and for recharging a notebook computer battery.
- With an extra layer of insulation on the floor, ceiling, and walls, rooms can be more energy efficient.
- Use every energy-saving option available (and affordable), such as a waterless toilet or low-flow showerhead.

- For new construction, use the more expensive high-efficiency windows throughout the home. For existing homes, install high-efficiency windows in rooms that are used more regularly. Close off the rooms that are not in use.
- Use an alternative fuel for heating, such as a solid biomass heater or a high-efficiency woodstove.
- Install hardwood floors instead of carpet, which can be very hard to clean and can also absorb light and sound.

NO MATTER HOW YOU CHOOSE TO CUT COSTS from your budget while making your home greener, your efforts will reduce your environmental footprint and save you money.

Action Points

The following action points are some ways to have a huge positive impact on your house-related bills and on the environment. Select one or two to start with and slowly implement more as you simplify your life.

1. Be more conscious of how you're using water while cooking, washing dishes and clothes, watering the lawn and garden, and showering. You may be surprised how quickly those gallons add up, especially when you start to calculate how many times you flush the toilet, rinse a dish off, and wash your hands.

2. Use appliances and electronics that are high efficiency or have power-saving features. Want to cut your gas bill? Change your furnace filter regularly, wash your clothes in warm or cold water rather than hot water, and mix foods into your diet that don't need to be cooked.

3. Some people think a larger house will cure their overcrowded-home syndrome. This is similar to believing that a crash diet will solve a weight problem. The true problem is out-of-control accumulation. Change your motives and lifestyle to achieve lifelong results.

4. If you live in a large home, using a primary room in the house is a great way to reduce heating, cooling, and electric bills.

5. Live in a smaller home. Not only will you have a greater impact on the environment, but you will have no place to put extra material things. Visit the Small House Society at ResourcesforLife.com/groups/smallhousesociety/ and learn more.

Discussion Questions

Here are some discussion questions for you, your roommate(s), spouse, family, friends, or book club to consider.

1. What are three practical changes you can make to how much water, electricity, and gas you use? What do you need to do to get started? Make a plan as to how you will accomplish this. How can you encourage someone else to reach and continue with his or her goal? How can that person encourage you?

2. Calculate how much money you can save next month if you make the three changes asked of you above. What will you do with the money you save?

3. What are some things you would enjoy about living in a large home? Are they things you could also enjoy in a small home? What are some things you can't do without? Think of how you could move into a smaller house while still keeping what you enjoy most. Talk with the people you live with and get their thoughts as well.

Your Plan

Now it's your turn to personalize this chapter. What will you do because of what you've read?

_____

_____

_____

_____

_____

_____

_____

_____

_____

_____

_____

_____

_____

_____

_____

_____

5

Traveling Green

He who
would travel
happily must
travel light.

—Antoine de Saint-Exupery

IN 1989, AFTER THE Exxon Valdez oil spill, all fingers were pointing to Exxon and placing the blame where one might expect. Surprisingly, Greenpeace launched an advertising campaign showing a photograph of the man in charge of the ship, Captain Joseph Hazelwood. Beneath his photo was the caption: "It wasn't his driving that caused the Alaskan oil spill. It was yours." That advertisement had an impact on me—perhaps because I was one who was quick to point the finger at Exxon without realizing or acknowledging my own participation in the spill. However, after seeing that ad I recognized that my own demand for oil was partly to blame for the spill. Yet, knowing this, I couldn't really think of an alternative to an automobile because I was dependent upon my car to live. My work depended upon me driving. The only change I could foresee making was a gradual long-term change in my life about how I would use transportation.

Transportation for Simpler and Smaller Living

I remember the day my dad told me that he could go from Iowa City to Des Moines (about a hundred miles) in less time riding a bicycle than it would take me driving a car. I'd grown accustomed to my dad thinking outside the box, but this statement just seemed too unbelievable. Then I listened as he explained his reasoning. "The time it takes to get somewhere in a car must include the operating cost of that vehicle and the time required on the job to earn the money for the purchase." He also explained that the time spent maintaining the car should also be considered, even while under warranty.

If it costs 50 cents per mile to operate a vehicle, then a hundred-mile ride in the car takes about two hours (in transit) and the amount of time required to earn

$50 to pay for the operation of the vehicle, and a portion of the time spent maintaining the car. For many people it might take a day or more to earn $50 (after taxes). So, someone starting out on their bicycle at ten miles per hour could leave Iowa City and arrive in Des Moines before a person could earn the money required to drive there. For this reason, the top speed of most automobiles is about ten miles per hour, since the more expensive the car, the "slower" it goes because we have to pay for it longer. Because of our instant-gratification culture, we are sheltered from these realities. Imagine if everyone were required to save up money to purchase a vehicle. If that were the case, we'd realize that the first mile we drive our new car actually takes about three to five years. Walking that mile would take about twenty minutes. Obviously, in rush-hour traffic and gridlock, driving a car is even less efficient.

It's not just the cost of a new vehicle that we should consider but also the opportunity cost of investing $20,000 to $30,000 in a depreciating asset rather than investing that money in a business or some interest-bearing account.

How much is your vehicle costing you? If you really consider the cost of payments, insurance, gas, oil changes, repairs, tires, emissions, and parking, the cost of owning an automobile is probably $300 to $400 per month for most people. What would you do with that kind of money left over each month?

For me, part of simple and small living involves simplicity in transportation. I very much want my choice of daily transportation to be as simple, small, and environmentally responsible as my home.

I sold my car on Earth Day in 2004 and began using a bike full-time, year-round.

Two technologies that make this possible are a good rain suit and a bike trailer for hauling larger loads. On the rare occasions that I need to use a car for out-of-town travel, I simply borrow or rent one, which over time ends up being much less expensive than owning a car. When I decided to live in a small house, I didn't want to make arrangements to store and maintain a car, so I decided that riding a bicycle year-round would be the way to go. Riding a bicycle is quiet. It saves time, money, and space. It doesn't pollute. Riding a bicycle is better for my community, the environment, and me.

Not having car expenses saves me about $300 per month.

I was driving a three-cylinder 1993 Geo Metro that got over forty miles per gallon. Since I put more than 200,000 miles on the car, the cost per mile declined considerably. However, most people don't drive ten-year-old cars, and they don't get that kind of mileage. The average person's car expenses are about $7,000 per year.

So what's the answer? How can we save time and money, and still have our transportation needs met? Here are some ideas, although it may require moving closer to work or using public transit.

Driving a Car

- Carpooling. How far away from home do you work? Five miles? Twenty-five miles? Do you know someone who lives close to you, has the same work schedule as you, and works near/with you? If it takes you an hour to get to work, and you have a coworker who lives fifteen minutes from your house—seven minutes from a halfway point—this person is the perfect carpool candidate. Set up a driving schedule and start counting all the money you'll be saving in gas, not to mention maintenance. If there is absolutely no one to carpool with to work, and your office is too far away to bike to, how else can you cut back on driving? Carpool to parties or sports practices. The more you share the cost of vehicle ownership, the more money you are saving. You can also check into telecommuting or working from home one day a week.

- Sharing a vehicle. Car sharing, as a commercial venture, is a fairly recent phenomenon. Companies like Zipcar and Flexcar are two examples. Car sharing can also be done on a smaller scale between several people. The insurance needs to include all drivers and some insurance companies may limit sharing. Let's say you are carpooling to work and sharing a vehicle with several other people. By organizing your errands, you've found that you can use a car just once a week to get all of your errands taken care of. Now that you are saving

The time it takes to get somewhere in a car must include the time required on the job to earn the money for the purchase and the operating cost of that vehicle.

money and time, what can you do to help the environment more? Be sure that your shared car is well maintained and as fuel efficient as possible.

➤ If you have two cars, could you survive with just one? If you have two cars and need two cars, primarily use the one with the best gas mileage. Buy a hybrid or a car that runs on an alternative fuel, not gasoline. For many people, their second car is a "car share" or flexcar vehicle (see "Sharing a vehicle" above). Other people are using electric cars of the class known as a neighborhood electric vehicle (NEV). These cars are all electric, very quiet, and low maintenance. They only travel at about twenty-five to thirty miles per hour and have a maximum travel distance of about fifty miles; however, this is typically plenty of speed and distance for most of the in-town driving that people do.

Riding a Bike

➤ Purchasing a bike. If you don't already own a bicycle, consider purchasing one from a locally owned and operated bicycle shop, where you can get personalized service to make sure you get a bike that fits your body and your needs. Small shops can also help keep the bike running in top condition. A basic bicycle may cost about $300 to $400 for the low-end models. There is a category of bicycles that are in the $1,000 range. The high end could be $2,000 or more for a racing-quality bike. If you want to purchase a previously owned bicycle, you might still consider stopping at the local bike shop and getting their advice. Let them know you'll be bringing the bicycle in for the initial and ongoing maintenance.

➤ Maintenance. One benefit of riding a bike instead of driving a car is that the maintenance seems less frequent, and it's certainly less expensive. If you've ever owned a car past the initial warranty period you know how expensive it can be from month to month keeping the vehicle running.

➤ Weather. I had been driving a car regularly for over ten years when I decided to switch back to a bicycle. In the past I had ridden as much as two hundred miles in two days; however, after a long time away from riding, it wasn't easy starting again. It was physically challenging (I was about sixty pounds overweight), and I also needed to figure out how to make it work in the rain and extreme cold. Something that really helped me enjoy year-round riding was discovering lightweight rain suits such as Frogg Toggs or Rainshield O2 Rainwear. I carry the rain suit with me at all times—that way I don't worry about the weather. If it begins to rain, I put the full-body suit on and stay dry. As long as I don't ride too hard, I actually find that the breeze helps me stay cool and comfortable in the hot Iowa summers. With a breathable rain suit and light layers of clothing, I can arrive at work refreshed and ready for the day.

➤ Trailers. Something else that helped me stick with biking was the ability to pull a small trailer behind the bike. This allowed me to carry items to work and do some grocery shopping. Trailers are between $200 and $300 for basic models.

➤ Safety. Some people are worried about weaving in and out of traffic. That's certainly something to be concerned about; however, many communities have bike lanes or separate bike trails for commuting. Also, neighborhood streets are sometimes quite direct and less traveled than main thoroughfares. I try to stay out of the heavy traffic. Commuting is a little more challenging than leisure riding. Sometimes you need to take routes that are not smooth, so a bike with some suspension can help soften the ride. Having really good brakes is essential.

➤ Stamina. After a few years of riding again, my stamina was better than ever. For a period of time I was biking regularly to a home I was house-sitting in the countryside that was about forty-five minutes away from the downtown area. On one occasion there were severe headwinds, and I had to ride up a steep hill in temperatures that were below zero, yet my body had adapted to the elements.

➤ Shopping. Some of your errands and shopping may take you places where there are no bicycle racks. Consider purchasing a "u-lock" design that immobilizes your bike. Many communities permit bicycles to be locked to parking meters or signs. With the bicycle trailer mentioned earlier, it's possible to carry a fairly large amount of groceries and other items. You'll certainly watch what you buy when space and weight are a consideration. If you have a long ride home

Public transportation systems are adapting to a society where more and more people use bicycles every day for their regular commuting.

and want to transport frozen or refrigerated products, carry a cooler with ice. Perhaps you've chosen to be a single-car family rather than a three-car family. Designate one person to be the driver and run the errands on a given day or in a certain week. Everyone else can run smaller errands and commute using bicycles.

Other Modes of Transportation

- Public transportation. Public transportation systems are adapting to a society where more and more people use bicycles every day for their regular commuting. Buses in some communities have bike racks on the front for carrying the bicycles of passengers who will ride the bike for errands or the remainder of their commute if it isn't covered by public transportation. If you ride a bus or use the subway, you then have extra time to read, listen to music, or meditate because someone else is driving.
- Walking. Walking is an excellent way to travel shorter distances. Some bicycle trailers include handles so they can double as walking trailers. These make it possible to walk with greater ease while transporting large or heavy loads. Walking allows people to engage in conversation more easily than when riding bicycles. Invest in a good pair of walking shoes or even street-running shoes (the kind with a very soft cushion sole). Sometimes walking can allow you to take routes that might not be available to a bicycle and certainly not to a car. Just as many cities ban skates and skateboards from sidewalks and other designated areas, some beautiful trails and parks do not permit bicycles but do permit pedestrians and hikers.
- Motorcycles. Although their fuel efficiency is attractive, motorcycles and scooters are not good choices for anyone concerned about survivability in an automobile accident.

Tips for Going Carless

If you really want to take the leap and sell your car for good, here are some things to keep in mind.

- Weather is unpredictable, and you could arrive to work, to the store, or to your job interview sweating or rain-soaked if you didn't plan ahead. It may be sunny in the morning, but by 5:00 p.m. it may be hailing. Always be prepared.
- Plan ahead if you know you will need a car, such as for a date, an errand day, or a road trip. Depending on who you are sharing a car with, you may need to reserve the car a week or more in advance.
- Be generous. If you are sharing a car that belongs to someone else, consider paying a minimum of 50 cents per mile, which is on the high end of what it costs to own and operate a vehicle.
- If a bicycle becomes your main source for transportation, don't let yourself get too vain that you don't wear a helmet. It's not only safe and smart to don a helmet but also a great way to promote bicycling. Carrying your helmet with you into stores and to your workplace sends a subliminal message that can quickly catch on.

NO MATTER HOW you choose to simplify your use of transportation, it can make an impact on your time, money, health, and the environment. Be open to new options until you find what will work best for you and also reduce your carbon footprint.

Remember that the small changes will have a greater impact in the long term, and you can make a positive impact in your life and the world around you.

Action Points

The following action points will help you know which transportation works best for your lifestyle. Select one or two to start with and slowly implement more as you simplify your life.

1. Contact your company to see if they have lists of existing carpools or find out if your coworkers would be interested in carpooling.
2. If your job is reasonably close to your home, or if you are just running errands, ride a bike or walk instead of using your car. This will save you time and money

and improve your health. Try it once or twice a week and then slowly build up to more days.

3. When you run errands, make sure you have planned out where you want to go to make the most of your transportation time and money.

4. If you are in a position to change the car you drive, try to find the most fuel-efficient vehicle for the lowest cost. Hybrid or electric cars may be more costly, but you may want to consider investing in one. They may save you money in the long run, as well as be better for the environment.

5. Find out if public transportation is a feasible option for you instead of driving your car.

Discussion Points

Here are some discussion points for you, your roommate(s), spouse, family, friends, or book club to consider.

1. How can you implement walking, riding your bike, and car sharing into your life? What do you need to do to get started? How can you and someone else help each other with your goals?

2. Challenge: Make a schedule so that you run all errands on one day of the week. Plan ahead. Think about what you need from the store for the entire week. Talk to a friend or family member and coordinate your schedules so that you can run errands together or pick something up for the other person while you're out. Share your experience with others who also have goals to drive less. How can you be better prepared for your next errand day?

3. For more about the real cost of transportation, visit travelmatters.org/calculator/individual/index. Discuss your findings.

Your Plan

Now it's your turn to personalize this chapter. What will you do because of what you've read?

_____

_____

_____

_____

_____

_____

_____

_____

_____

_____

_____

_____

_____

_____

_____

6

Technology Is Shrinking Our Lives

Science and technology multiply around us.
To an increasing extent they dictate the languages
in which we speak and think. Either we use
those languages, or we remain mute.

—J. G. Ballard

Technology: Environmental Enemy or Ally?

SOME ENVIRONMENTALISTS reject technology because they believe technology and industrialization threaten our planet. Perhaps you hold this view. For a long time, I too believed that technological advancement and nature were at odds with each other. While industrialized nations have some comforts and conveniences not found in developing nations, they are also facing some of the greatest challenges with water, air, and land pollution—despite government oversight and the efforts of environmental groups. This is because per-capita consumption and consumerism is typically higher among industrialized nations. As a result, air pollution in some metropolitan areas presents a serious health threat. Given the negative externalities of industry and development, I once concluded that for us to truly be in harmony with nature, we would need to give up all technology and use wind power to pump water, lanterns for light, and horses and buggies for travel.

However, what I have since discovered, is that technology such as a notebook computer has allowed me to use less power and shrink my life, placing less demand on the natural resources of our planet. Because my cell phone and notebook computer run on battery power, I can comfortably live in a home that doesn't have electricity. Low-power appliances and gadgets are not just a benefit to those living off the grid. If you currently spend $150 a month on an electric bill, how would you like to see that drop to $50 a month or even $25 a month? The technological options available today are much broader than just replacing some incandescent light bulbs with compact fluorescent.

In some ways, technology has, in fact, allowed me to live a more austere lifestyle. I don't have a horse and buggy, yet my bicycle has become a more viable alternative to the car.

I can carry everything I need in my notebook computer stored in a backpack.

When I want to travel light, a USB memory stick (the size of a pack of gum) allows me to carry several filing cabinets worth of documents around with me. Today a USB memory stick serves the purpose that floppy diskettes did twenty years ago; however, a USB memory stick can hold the equivalent of almost 3,000 diskettes of information (for a 4GB memory stick). These storage devices come in various sizes and range in price from about $15 (for the low-capacity units) to about $100 or more (for the higher-capacity units). This tiny device can store the documents that might have previously cluttered your desk.

With an increased global population placing greater demand on this earth's limited natural resources, technology also opens up avenues for communication that can save on print and travel costs. For example, on July 7, 2007, the ResourcesForLife.com conference was held in Iowa City. A small number of people attended the live event; however, through the use of the Internet, thousands of people have now listened to and viewed the presentations that were given that day. This dramatically reduced the environmental impact of the event. Increasingly, people are using video conferencing and e-mail as an alternative to traveling for face-to-face meetings.

As an information technology consultant, much of the information commerce I engage in is in digital form. As such, there is no physical package for the products and services I buy and sell, so this has a positive impact on the environment. Technology should serve us and not the other way around. As we learn to more effectively leverage the available technology in our lives, we will be able to free up time, money, and space, replacing unnecessary clutter with time for family, friends, fitness, and other things that we enjoy.

Going Digital

I've come to see technology as a wonderful means for downsizing my living space. As we increasingly enter into an information age, more of our possessions take on a digital form. Think about your own purchases over the last couple of years. Maybe you've gone from buying music on CDs to purchasing downloaded music online. Are you someone who goes online to receive bank statements and pay bills? Is your photography collection now inside your computer rather than in photo albums on shelves? Is your list of names and phone numbers in your cell phone rather than written in a book? These are all examples of how individuals are slowly transforming the information in their lives from physical form into digital. As a result of this trend, businesses are also forced to adjust. For example, in some areas, such as college towns like Iowa City, music stores selling audio CDs are harder to find, since many younger people are downloading their music. By early 2008, Apple had sold over four billion song downloads through the iTunes online music, video, and media store.

In fact, now you can store music, photographs, feature films, homemade videos, books, correspondence, and other personal items in computers, which take up very little space. For some people, the pocket-sized video iPod, or a similar device, has replaced the television, photo album, and stereo system. Documents are available in electronic form or, if printed, can easily be scanned and stored in electronic form. These developments have made it possible to downsize without getting rid of what we care about.

Plant a Tree for Me

The computer manufacturer Dell is doing more than just selling computers. Through their "Plant a Tree for Me" program, consumers can request that trees be planted with or without the purchase of a computer to help offset the impact of computers on the environment. To learn more, simply do a Google search on Dell and Plant a Tree for Me.

Once documents are in digital form, they are much easier to move around, sort, organize, copy, backup, and search. For example, a software program called PaperPort, included with auto-feeding Visioneer scanners, will quickly scan in all of your receipts and other paperwork, read it, index it, and then allow you to quickly search through thousands of on-screen pages. Trying to find that receipt from last year? Simply type in the name of the merchant or any other uniquely identifiable information on the receipt, and it will come up instantly on the screen.

Another factor contributing to the shrinking of our lives into digital form is convergence—several pieces of equipment merged into one device. The notebook computer is an example of this.

In something typically less than one inch thick is a complete computer system with keyboard, display, and processor.

Another example of convergence is the popular all-in-one printer, scanner, copier, and fax machine. Many of these come with a memory card reader for digital cameras as well. Machines that used to take up significant amount of space on a desktop are now combined into one multifunctional device not much bigger than a small microwave oven or bread box (if you remember what that is).

In addition to convergence we are seeing smaller devices. When convergence meets miniaturization, something really amazing happens. On June 29, 2007, Apple introduced the iPhone pocket computer, which combines numerous areas of life into a pocket-size device: e-mail, telephone, Internet, pager, camera, telephone book, calendar, weather report, contacts, maps, television, audio books, radio, movies, music videos, music, photographs, and more. As of early 2008, the system is available with 8GB of storage, which means there is room to store over ten thousand pages of text. The iPhone does about 90 percent of what I need to do on a computer, so when I'm at home, this pocket-size device replaces an entire room full of equipment. I still use a notebook computer for video production, audio editing, and Web site design. However, my other daily tasks are easily done on the smaller, more energy efficient, and more reliable iPhone. By January 2008, over four million iPhones had been sold in about six months—an average of 20,000 purchased per day.

The price for smaller products is also shrinking. The computer manufacturer Asus offers the two-pound Eee PC notebook for about $400. The system runs on the Linux operating system rather than Microsoft Windows. To learn more, do a Google search on Asus Eee PC or go to the eeepc.asus.com Web site.

Computer Accessories for Smaller Living

The space-saving benefits of any single piece of technology by itself might not seem that significant; however, the collective use of a few gadgets and accessories can significantly reduce the living space a person needs. In the office, an all-in-one printer combined with a notebook computer can make it possible to run an entire business in a space about the same size as a walk-in closet.

Photos

In recent years, I was inspired by a friend to become interested in digital scrapbook making. She is a real pro at it, and by switching over to digital manipulation, I have saved an incredible amount of time and money as well as having become more environmentally conscientious by not contributing to the chemical and paper waste of

Going Paperless

In the information age, items such as bank statements, invoices, receipts, newsletters, owner manuals, correspondence, and other documents are available in electronic form. This saves paper waste in your home and in the environment. Here are some examples and bits of advice:

- Avoid getting sucked into free samples, free magazines, or free newspapers that create more waste. Free e-mail newsletters are better for the environment than paper format, but they still take up your time. The best thing to do is consider what you really need before signing up.
- Use a PDA (personal digital assistant), like a PalmPilot, iPhone, or Windows Mobile device instead of a day planner or a calendar.
- Ask for electronic bank statements, credit card bills, and utility bills rather than hard copy.
- Scan, file, shred, and recycle paper documents after you have used them. The PaperPort software that comes with Visioneer scanners will read every document scanned. The words are recognized and indexed, so finding a piece of paper is as easy as having the computer search for some words that are on that paper.
- Fast duplex scanners such as the Fujitsu ScanSnap make it possible to quickly scan and digitize hundreds of pages in very little time. A duplex scanner quickly scans both sides of a page at the same time. In this way, the computer file created can offer viewing of multiple pages.

photographic processing. I also don't have to worry about storing any photo albums because they are all saved in my computer.

How many photo albums do you have? I know some people with shelves of photos, or even closets filled with boxes of photos, slides, and/or home movies. Not only are these areas of wasted space, but these items are degrading in quality over time because of dust and decay.

Existing photo albums, scrapbooks, slides, negatives, and photos can be scanned into digital format.

Once these items are scanned, they can be stored on a CD or DVD, and a copy can easily be placed in a safe location such as a safe-deposit box at the bank, ensuring that those valuable family photos won't be permanently lost or damaged. If you have a good scanner, you can take the time to scan in photos yourself, but it's also possible to have your old slides and photos digitized by a photo company for a relatively low cost. I know of someone who had two thousand slides they needed scanned. Rather than doing this on their own, they hired someone to do it. Their many boxes of slides were reduced to a single DVD. Once you have all of your photos in digital format, you need to decide if you should permanently get rid of the physical photos or make sure they are properly stored against deterioration. Some people will choose to keep their original slides, negatives, or prints, but the digital version becomes what they enjoy, work with, and share on a regular basis.

The expanded availability of digital cameras has made it possible to take thousands of pictures and share them with friends and family using e-mail or by posting them on the Internet. By having a Web site or online journal, you can share photos of your life's adventures with the world. With online photo sharing, services such as Google's Picasa Web Albums allow you to provide captions, keywords, and even a mapping feature that shows satellite photos of where your photos were taken. Taking photographs with a digital camera is also a wonderful substitute for collecting larger sentimental things. You can take pictures of the items you love but don't really need and then put those photos in a digital scrapbook instead of storing the unneeded objects. The scrapbooks are like a photo journal and time-line of your life.

For those who haven't made the switch to a digital camera, you can request that your photos be processed and placed on a CD rather than ordering prints. Or you can request both prints and a CD. However, having the photos in a digital format can be a great help. The cost of taking the pictures and transferring them from CD to a computer is minimal, and if you have the scrapbook pages already in place, it is simple enough to print them out. Paying for the few prints that you really want is much more economical because you aren't wasting time, money, and space through the process of taking, processing, and storing physical prints.

Journals and Books

By journaling our daily, weekly, or monthly experiences, we can convert our life into writing. Digital journaling provides the same advantages of digital photos. You can save multiple files on your computer instead of having stacks of journals taking up space. The ink and paper used on journals can also experience deterioration over time, whereas a digital copy can be safely stored and easily searched.

In addition to journaling, consider downsizing the amount of movies and books that you purchase. Libraries and rental stores are a great source for videos. Services such as Netflix allow you to have access to a library of many thousands of videos without needing to own them. Instead of buying a movie after you have seen it, consider writing a short review of it while the plot is still fresh in your mind. That way you can remember what you enjoyed about it. You can also do the same thing with books that you have read. Some people collect books, not for use, but simply for the sake of having books. If you are a collector of books, consider replacing the majority of your books with short reviews or journal entries. Keep only your absolute favorite reads. Wikipedia is a collaborative online encyclopedia of reference information available for free. This and other online information have largely replaced in-home libraries of reference material. Google Books now offers full text of many public domain books. The sacred-texts.com Web site offers over 1,400 books online for free in searchable text. The collection is also available on DVD for under $100 and has over 124,000 files. Here are a few suggestions for getting control over the books and other texts in your life.

> Were there quotes that you like from the book? Was there something about a relationship in the storyline that you admired?

Instead of buying a movie after you have seen it, consider writing a short review of it while the plot is still fresh in your mind. That way you can remember what you enjoyed about it.

- What was it that you got out of the book? Can that be written down and condensed?
- Is the same information available online or in a PDF format?
- Could you just rely on the local library for some of the books you currently have in your collection? Consider donating books to a local organization's library or public library to make them available for you and others to enjoy.

Another thing to consider is that books are becoming more available in digital format, which you can download to a home computer or iPod. This allows you to still enjoy your favorite form of entertainment without cluttering up your home. If you are interested in the content of a book and don't necessarily care about reading it, audio books are an alternative to printed books.

Music and Movies

The introduction of the iPod and the iTunes store from Apple was a very significant development. The iTunes store was announced at a time when the music industry was in the midst of a crisis. Millions of music lovers were "sharing the love" illegally by digitizing their music collections and making them available for free with file sharing over the Internet. At the height of this pirating extravaganza, Steve Jobs made a monumental announcement that initially seemed absurd. He suggested that people purchase music rather than get it for free. Why would people purchase something that was available for free? At the unveiling of the iTunes online store, Jobs explained that people would pay because the music they would purchase would be high quality, easy to find, easy to download, and would come with accurate album information including the original album art. Jobs also declared that it is "bad karma" to steal. A speculative world waited and then was amazed as the iTunes store became a huge success. It seemed that Jobs's "thou shall not steal" proclamation (or reiteration) was received and honored by the people. It was as much a landmark event for morality as it was for technology. From that day on, it became possible for people to build a music collection including hundreds of albums that could be stored on a computer or even in a pocket. This was a big advancement for small living. I know that my CD collection previously took up many bookshelves. Now that the Apple iTunes store offers audio books, television shows, movies, and other media, the need to physically store DVDs and other items has been eliminated. Old CDs and DVDs can be given to a local public library or donated to local thrift stores that raise money for socially beneficial work and relief efforts.

It's not uncommon to spend $15 or $20 on a CD or DVD. These can be purchased online and downloaded for $10 to $15.

As of January 2008, it became possible to rent movies directly from the Apple iTunes store for about $3 or $4.

For people who typically watch a movie once and never again, this is a way to save money and storage space. In addition to saving money at the time of purchase, the downloaded files don't scratch or get lost (assuming you make backups). The process of downloading audio books, music, or videos is quite simple. Using the free iTunes software program, a person can go to the online store and search using a variety of methods to find just what they are looking for. Helpful suggestions for other purchases are also provided. When you purchase music, you will be given a list of other music that you might like based on what you are buying. Quite often, these suggestions are surprisingly accurate. Podcasts are audio and video broadcasts that are usually provided for free. So, not all of your media needs to be expensive. With iTunes it is also possible to transfer an entire CD collection into the computer. Automatically, iTunes adds the cover art for the music to your computer using a free online database of CD album cover art. Lyrics that normally would be included with a CD are now available online. With a little effort, you can save the lyrics with the MP3 audio file and store them with the song in iTunes. To do this, just perform a Google search for a phrase that you heard in the song. Put that phrase in quotes when you search and then include the word lyrics after the words in quotes. I've used this method to find songs when I didn't know the artist or song name, but only heard the last few seconds of a song.

Some very good music is available for free from artists who want their work to be in the public domain or protected by the Creative Commons license. Web sites like kahvi.org help promote the work of such musicians. Songs can be downloaded for free and a complete collection of music can be ordered on DVD for a small price. The Web site jazz-on-line.com allows users to download over 19,000 jazz titles that are in the public domain. The cost for three months unlimited access is $5 to help cover Web site hosting costs.

Video and Music Production

Not too many years ago, a music recording studio or a video editing and production studio would have required a large room and a considerable investment. Apple was one of the first manufacturers to offer video production to the at-home computer user, saving considerable space and money. Their iLife software makes it possible to produce very high-quality DVD media. In 2006, Apple introduced a music composition system and multitrack digital recorder called Garage Band. Today, using the Apple iLife suite of products, you can integrate video, music, and photography for under $100. All of this can be done using a very slim notebook. A computer using Microsoft Windows can also perform these tasks, although the available software is generally more expensive and more complicated to use.

Web Site

For little or no money and a small investment of time, you can create and maintain your own Web site. Services like Blogger by Google are free and provide a searchable repository for writings and reference information. I use my own Web site, ResourcesforLife.com, as an online encyclopedia of information that I go back to frequently. It's like having my own Wikipedia I can send people to when they have questions about a topic I've already researched and written about. You probably have something you are passionate about. You may have considered it a hobby. Yet, after years of experience, you've become somewhat of an expert, and now family, friends, and colleagues ask you for help. A Web site can be an excellent way to share your knowledge.

A Web site can also be an organized directory of links to information that is otherwise spread around on the Internet and often difficult to locate when you want it again. Increasingly my "possessions" are shared information resources. They are part of the collective creative commons of society. For example, I may have contributed to an entry in Wikipedia, but I don't own it. It is owned by society. So, I might simply have a link to that writing. That way I can easily refer back to it when needed. Rather than having information resources in hard copy, we have easy access through a personalized Web site to the information that we collectively share. Ownership of tangible goods reinforces the finite availability of a durable good. Yet information resources are easily shared. As we move increasingly into an information society, it will be easier to have equitable distribution of information (the new wealth) and education—making it possible for all people to become empowered. This is the vision of organizations like One Laptop Per Child (OLPC). For more information visit the laptop.org Web site.

Tips for Utilizing Technology

In many ways, technology has made smaller living more possible today than ever before. Here are some examples to get you thinking about how to save space, time, and money.

- Replace your VCR/DVD player with a notebook computer that will handle your multimedia needs.
- Consider purchasing a projection system to be used on occasions when you want to have a theater experience. When not in use, it can be easily stored away.
- Replace your clock/radio/alarm/phone/CD player with a pocket-size convergence device such as an iPhone that serves all of these tasks. With a small yet powerful set of speakers, such a device can replace your home stereo.
- If you use a tape recorder, consider replacing it with a pocket-size digital recorder.
- Convert all old home videos, photos, audiocassettes, records, documents, and other media to digital format. Software such as RecordNow by Roxio can help convert your old cassette tapes and vinyl records to digital format. The software can remove scratches or hiss from the recording. You'll simply need the appropriate cables to connect your stereo components to the computer. To learn more, do a Google search for Roxio RecordNow.
- Consider replacing AC-powered devices with DC-battery devices that can be recharged. These are typically smaller and more efficient. If you're using smaller battery-powered portable devices, you will find that you can easily carry the device throughout your home. A notebook computer is a good example of this. It is smaller and requires less power to operate than a regular desktop computer. Because it is portable, it can serve as both a home and an office computer.

GOING DIGITAL DOESN'T MEAN you have to give up the familiar things in life. I still have bank statements, photo albums, movies, television shows, music, books, and other things as I did before. It's just that now they are in digital form. In some respects, my life appears on the outside to reflect a dramatic transition, yet in reality it hasn't changed much. I'm just making the best use of available technology and also downsizing the amount of resources I use, which helps me lessen my environmental impact.

Action Points

The following action points are some ways to have technology help you save time, money, and space. Select one or two to start with and slowly implement more as you simplify your life.

1. Invest in multifunctional pieces of equipment such as an all-in-one printer or pocket computers instead of buying individual pieces of equipment that can take up more space.

2. If you have the resources for it, invest in good scanning equipment and programs to help you downsize the amount of paper and photographs in your home. If this isn't an option for you, look into outsourcing your scanning needs.

3. Look into digital scrapbook making. There are programs you can buy or download off the Internet to help you set up templates. Once those templates are in place, it becomes a simple process of filling in the existing spaces with your digital photos.

4. Download your existing DVDs and CDs onto your computer or iPod, and then donate the originals to a charity organization. This way you can simplify your space as well as contribute to your community.

5. Become the media. Today's media is filled with sensationalism and misinformation. Consider creating your own Web page with news or helpful information from firsthand experience. If you enjoy writing, start a mailing list. Even without sophisticated technology, you can offer your knowledge and experience to others. If you produce videos, offer these as an alternative to television programming.

Discussion Questions

Here are some discussion questions for you, your roommate(s), spouse, family, friends, or book club to consider.

1. Online conferencing, discussion groups, collaboration, conference calls, and e-mail are all examples of how to utilize technology and also save on travel costs. How are you currently using technology to help you save time, money, and space? What are some examples of how these technologies could be used by your family or in the workplace?

2. If you aren't familiar with using equipment such as laptops, PDAs, cell phones, or other technological gadgets, are there people in your life who are more technologically savvy than you who could help you find equipment that could simplify your life? List at least five people and call one of them today.

Your Plan

Now it's your turn to personalize this chapter. What will you do because of what you've read?

_____

_____

_____

_____

_____

_____

_____

_____

_____

_____

_____

_____

_____

_____

_____

_____

7

How Small Will You Go?

Live simply
that others
might simply
live.

—Elizabeth Seaton

THE RESPONSES from around the world to my tiny home have been over-whelmingly positive. It's actually quite surprising, since just about anything today can become controversial with people on either side of any issue. Yet in the four years I've been living in my home, I can recall only one person who was negative about it. That person stated that people living a normal life wouldn't be able to live in a smaller home. They didn't know me well enough to realize that I actually live a very normal life with a regular day job and a full schedule of activities.

If you're thinking about beginning the journey of moving into a smaller home, there are some things you'll want to consider ahead of time. Because it is a process, you may end up being partway through the journey and then have regrets. So, as much as possible, consider all that's involved. Some of what I will be discussing is applicable to everyone regardless of the size of their living space. Don't think you have to change your lifestyle all at once or that you have to simplify as far as I did. The key is to find what works best for you and your loved ones. Consider renting a small space about the same size you are thinking about building or buying. Try it out for a few months, or a few years, before making a larger commitment.

Things I Miss

Living in my very small home, I miss having a guest room and the amenities most guests would want such as a bathroom, shower, and full-size kitchen. I've considered building another small house as a guesthouse, because I like the idea of having an extra room if a friend or family member wants to spend the night. As an alternative when people come to visit, I treat them with a stay at a local bed-and-breakfast. I enjoy cooking, entertaining, and being hospitable, so it'd be nice to be able to invite friends over if I had access to a full-size kitchen and dining area. My dining table folds out and can accommodate two people, but I usually meet friends downtown at a restaurant instead. When the weather is nice, the park is available for a larger gathering of family or friends. Ideally, were my house to be part of a larger community of tiny homes, we could all share a community center with a large kitchen, a dining area, a living room, laundry facilities, exercise facilities, restroom facilities, and showers. At present, these resources are all within a short bicycle ride of my home.

Significant Other

I've often advised people who are considering marriage to put themselves through an intentionally stressful or challenging circumstance. I once spent a week riding a bicycle across the state of Iowa with a woman I'd started dating. Extreme heat, tropical downpours, mud, cramped sleeping quarters, physical exhaustion, and other factors pushed us to the breaking point, yet it didn't strain our relationship. We had a great time, laughed through it all, and came away from the experience even closer. So it is with sharing a tiny home with someone. It will either bring you closer together or magnify your differences to the point you won't be able to stand each other.

Perhaps people considering marriage should spend some extended time in a tiny house to see how compatible they are.

I was worried that living in an unusually small and somewhat quirky home might put an end to my social life, particularly dating, but I've been pleasantly surprised to find that my social life has expanded since moving into my tiny home. Most people I've met since moving into my small home have had a very positive reaction, perhaps because of the endearing cottagelike appearance. I find that having a somewhat quirky house is actually a good point of conversation. It's small, so sharing the space definitely makes time together more cozy. Tiny homes are ideally suited for one to two very compatible and very minimalist people. People with an inner contentment who are calm, meditative, and peaceful will likely do well in tiny homes; however, small homes may present a challenge for people who are restless and fidgety. People who are regularly looking outward for activities, products, foods, and experiences to bring them a sense of contentment may find a smaller home a bit confining—or at least they might not be able to spend too much time there before becoming bored.

If two people are currently married and considering a tiny home, they need to consider how compatible they are when sharing a smaller space.

Some couples are able to spend hours together without getting on each other's nerves; other couples have found that they really need separate spaces in order to maintain harmony in their relationship.

This may be the result of personality differences, or it might be a result of different styles of keeping spaces (messy or tidy). Couples who need separate spaces might consider two tiny houses. One house could be the office or daytime work area for one of the people in the relationship.

Experiment living in a small space and keep a journal of your impressions. It seems to me that most of us are not accustomed to journaling on a regular basis; yet journaling is an essential part of understanding the present and past of our personal life. It can give us a more objective "God's-eye view" of patterns, trends, and pitfalls, as well as the ability to see cause and effect. Consider living in a small space for a short period of time as an experiment. Pick one room in your home or apartment and let it be your "everything room" along with the bathroom. See how well you do in the "everything room." Try making it into a sparse space and then try filling it up. How does it feel? What are your goals? Do you want to save money? Do you want to save time? Are you trying to create a certain feeling in the space where you will spend much of your life? Is the new living space improving your exercise routine? How is it impacting your relationships? Are you sleeping better? What do your friends and family think of your new space? Do you care what they think?

Consider living in a small space for a short period of time as an experiment. Pick one room in your home or apart- ment and let it be your "everything room" along with the bathroom.

During the experiment, consider how you can make your daily routine run smoother. Perhaps you'll find that it's easier to have a place for everything and everything in its place when you have fewer things. Plan your living space proactively, rather than reacting and letting clutter take over.

Family

When considering an ideal home for a family, it's important to recognize that children typically are not content to sit and do nothing for hours on end. It's one thing for an adult to choose simple and small surroundings as a way of life, but children may find it very difficult to adjust to not having space to run around and play. A sizeable assortment of toys and books helps stimulate learning and growth. Sharing parks, playgrounds, and recreation facilities can help reduce the size of your home—you certainly need a balance when seeking a space that's sufficient and economically practical. In the summer, the outdoors can be a great place for kids to play and let off steam; however, in the winter, with shorter days, the home ends up serving as an indoor playground. For these reasons, it would seem that an extremely tiny home may not meet the needs of children. While a crib in the parents' room is suitable for an infant, adolescents and teens have a need for independence and privacy.

It seems that there could be a correlation between the bloating of homes in North America and the increase in health problems and divorce rates. It's known that financial problems and related stress are the number one cause of divorce. We know that large homes create a financial strain on young married couples. The time and money spent on larger homes results in less time and money for the needs of fitness and relationship maintenance. For this reason, I see smaller and more economical living spaces as a solution to the national health crisis, indebtedness, and problem of divorce.

Smaller homes and communities designed to support them are more family friendly than sprawling urban centers.

Clusters of smaller homes are sometimes equated with the squalor of poor shanty-towns. In such illegal squatter camps, homes are typically made of plywood, corrugated metal, and sheets of plastic. In these densely populated close quarters, the spread of disease is likely. Unfortunately, this is the image many people have of small home communities. However, it is possible to have beautiful communities of smaller homes where houses are made of quality materials and the necessary utilities are available to offer clean water, trash and waste removal, and other city services.

An alternative for young families would be to join or establish a cottage community. In this cottage community, the "homes" would simply offer restrooms, sleep accommodations, and a small kitchen. Other family activities could be in a shared community center where children could play. Perhaps the community center could also serve as a school and day care for the families in the community. This kind of model for living is popular in other countries, such as Kibbutz-style living found in Israel.

Children enjoy playing with pets and are often the reason why a family seeks to have a pet. With a shared community center, it would be possible to have cats, dogs, and other pets that would be part of the community. These pets could live independent of any family, which would reinforce the concept that they are independent living beings and not property that is owned. The feeding and care of these pets could be shared—something that requires much time and expense. Pet sitting wouldn't be necessary because there would always be a family to care for the pets. Neglect or lack of affection wouldn't be an issue either with so many people around.

Families wanting a smaller home without access to a cottage community could consider having the living room serve multiple purposes as a dining room, play room, family room, and office.

Small House Mobility

My home is on a street-legal trailer complete with lights and a license plate. Because the home weighs about 3,000 pounds, a heavy-duty truck is needed to pull it. I originally envisioned placing it in different locations over time to enjoy a variety of venues such as the ocean, a lake, or the mountains; however, it has remained on the same property for over three years. With today's very mobile society, it would be wonderful if, with the investment most people make in their homes, they could take their house with them if their next job is in another town.

Small House Camping

Small moveable cabins would be ideal for people who enjoy hunting, fishing, camping, or bird watching. Although I'm not a hunter, I enjoy the outdoors and certainly appreciate the conservation efforts of the many people who enjoy hunting and fishing. A tiny home on wheels has an advantage over an RV or camper in that the materials used are residential or commercial grade, and for that reason they are more suitable for year-round use. Recreational camping is typically seasonal. For this reason, some campers are built with lightweight materials, since they are anticipated to be used as fair-weather recreational vehicles. For people who hunt or fish in the colder winter months, it is essential to have shelter that can be used in severe weather.

When to Stop Living Small

As long as I'm single or dating I plan to live this way. For many years I was renting a small space and found it perfectly adequate. I'm better off owning the equivalent of a small free-standing efficiency apartment. In this way, I build equity, and now that the home is paid for, the money I would be spending on housing can now be redirected in other ways. Were I to get married, I would want a home that meets the needs and interests of the woman I would be with.

Finances

Now that I have very few living expenses, people imagine that I have plenty of extra cash; yet this isn't the case. I have just shifted my monthly expenses into more financially rewarding areas, such as investing in my own business, rather than paying rent to enrich the net worth of a landlord. Usually when people come to me for financial help, I give them suggestions and strategies about how to better manage their finances and create wealth in their life. That's the only thing that can truly help. Those who want quick cash generally won't listen, and regardless of how much money I give them, they seem to return to the same state of poverty. Those who sincerely want to change will listen to my advice, put it into practice, and benefit.

A criticism that people sometimes have of businesses is that many are looking at the bottom line and letting money determine business decisions. In doing so, businesses run the risk of not having a moral compass or higher purpose. The

With today's very mobile society, it would be wonderful if, with the investment most people make in their homes, they could take their house with them if their next job is in another town.

same is true for individuals. We should let our principles and values determine how we use our time, money, and space. Our decisions should not purely be based upon money.

An example would be in the purchase of office equipment. Many institutions will request bids and then purchase from the vendor with the lowest price. In the long run, the lowest-priced item may be the item of greatest cost to own and operate. For this reason, money really can't be a primary factor in decision making. Similarly, in life it's best to consider what enhances our relationships, provides us with greater health, builds up our careers, and provides us with long-term financial well-being. This is a holistic approach to decision making.

Sometimes an item of lesser cost will provide the greatest performance, but that is not always the case. The Web site consumerreports.org is a great source for evaluations of products. In many instances, the highest-ranked product is among the least expensive. One principle to consider is to seek quality in all things—in relationships, in work, in food, in rest, in play, and in all areas of life. Purchase what you can afford, but seek after quality. For example, in my opinion, if you have enough money for a very inexpensive but unreliable car or a very nice bicycle, consider purchasing the bicycle. It's better to have a high-quality bicycle than a poor-quality vehicle. Perhaps you can afford a very run-down and poorly constructed large home, or a very beautiful well-constructed small home. It's better to have the smaller home, because it is of better quality.

When you are living smaller and simpler, people will stop giving you gifts that need to be stored, dusted, and cared for.

Instead, you can request that gifts be consumables, such as food or product categories you currently use.

What are your priorities in life? Are you spending your money in ways that reflect those priorities? Is your spending balanced? Does your spending enrich every area of your life—relationships, health, education, career, donations? The journey toward holistic financial well-being is a process that takes time. Making choices for more-affordable quality items in your life will help establish wealth in your life. Being surrounded by fewer, higher-quality things will impact your life and inspire you to have quality in all that you do. Debts are like a leak in your gas tank. They continue to diminish your wealth even while you sleep. By contrast, investments increase your wealth while you sleep, so pay off your debts and invest. Having a simpler, smaller home should even save you money on homeowner's insurance. For donating money to charity, research what organizations are most effective with your contributions. Go to the following Web site for a list of online resources: ResourcesforLife.com/groups/financial.

A Last Word on Time

Once you're into your new lifestyle, don't forget that you will have more time on your hands, too. Treat it as you would money and really weigh your options of how to use your days and weeks. What have you always wanted to do? What makes you the happiest? What are you most afraid of or horrible at? Horseback riding? Rock climbing? Roller-skating? Public speaking? Singing? Set goals and come up with a plan of attack.

Each person's living situation is different. What's feasible for one person might not be for another. The important thing is that you start taking a look at your priorities and figure out what will best fit the lifestyle you envision for yourself. Remember that you can make positive changes to simplify your life, and in return, you will be blessed with more time, more money, better health, and a smaller environmental footprint, which impacts everyone. Believe that you can do it. Change can be hard at first, but if you make a plan and follow through with it, I guarantee that your life will improve for the better.

Action Points

The following action points can help you get started toward smaller living.
1. Create a tiny home within your home as a short-term experiment to learn more about how you feel in a smaller space.
2. As you shop, or replace items you currently own, choose smaller alternatives. Create a list of smaller items you want to replace or purchase. Include a plan for donating or selling your old items.

Discussion Questions

Here are some discussion questions for you, your roommate(s), spouse, family, friends, or book club to consider.

1. Have you ever lived in a sparse or small space? How did that make you feel?
2. What are some potential drawbacks to smaller and simpler living? What solutions can you think of to overcome those challenges?
3. What are you willing to give up to live smaller? What can't you live without?

Begin the First Chapter of Your Plan

Now it's your turn to start down a new path. What are you going to do today, tomorrow, and in the future to put your life on a diet?

_____

_____

_____

_____

_____

_____

_____

_____

_____

_____

_____

_____

_____

_____

_____

_____

_____

_____

Resources
for
Simple Living

Out of intense
complexities,
intense simplicities
emerge.

—**Winston Churchill**

THERE ARE numerous resources for simpler and smaller living at the Small House Society Web site found at ResourcesforLife.com. This chapter provides an abbreviated list of resources from this Web site. There is also a discussion group online and a monthly e-mail newsletter.

Books

There are many books on small houses available through the Resources for Life online store, where you'll find a complete selection of books on cabins, log homes, decorating small, modern designs, tree houses, design, construction, and the Not So Big series by Sarah Susanka. The bookstore can be found by visiting astore.amazon.com/resourcesforlife.

A few books are highlighted below, which are also available directly from the authors, whom I've come to know over the past few years. Except for Jay Shafer's book, the descriptions provided are from the Resources for Life store (hosted by Amazon).

Living SMALL:
The Life of Small Houses
Dennis Fukai

Living SMALL: The Life of Small Houses is an innovative book about the value of living in a small purposeful house. The book is a graphic narrative written in the comic style that mixes layers of visual information with interactive 3D computer models of twenty small houses. These small houses include early shelters, settler cabins, Cracker houses, farmhouses, bandboxes, shotguns, bungalows, and very tiny houses. Each house has a lesson to teach on how to live simply and purposefully in an efficient and multifunctional space. The book's CD includes the SketchUp Viewer, the construction information models, and a detailed help menu that readers can use to orbit, enter, and visualize each of the small houses. Students, homeowners, and building professionals will recognize the evolution of small houses into a consumer-oriented housing market and understand the purposeful nature of a small, simple, and sustainable shelter in an ever-changing world.

Little House on a Small Planet: Simple Homes, Cozy Retreats, and Energy Efficient Possibilities
Shay Salomon

"I cannot recommend this book highly enough. For anyone who has ever dreamed of getting off the mortgage rat race and creating not just a house, but a cozy nest that fits—this is the book! Every page is an inspiration, filled with real-life stories and lessons learned on creating better, more affordable, sustainable, and very personalized housing. There is something here that will fit nearly every lifestyle. For those who want to live in a better way: Read this book!"

—Janet Luhrs, author of *The Simple Living Guide and Simple Loving*, and publisher of *Simple Living Oasis*

"Salomon offers the savviest plan I've read for figuring out what house you really need . . . Her questions have forced me to rethink so much."

—Marta Salij, *Detroit Free Press*

From the Back Cover

Live in less space but have more room to enjoy it. Does that sound like a contradiction? Smart readers will discover that, on the contrary, living small can free up your mind, your wallet, and your soul. With the cost of living rising, and the environment suffering from excessive building, now is the time to scale back. Join the movement.

Little House on a Small Planet is a guidebook and an invitation. With floor plans, photographs, advice, and anecdotes, this unique book asks and answers, "What fills a home when the excess is cut away, and how do we get there from here?"

Pockets of people all over the continent are realizing the benefits of scaling down. You too can build a joyful, sane life that emphasizes home life over home maintenance. To get more information on how to live simply visit littlehouseonasmallplanet.com.

The Small House Book
Jay Shafer

This 4" x 5" three-volume set presents the economic, environmental, and social merits of compact housing with dozens of color photos on a 95-page layout. It also describes the principles and processes of designing a tiny house of one's own. Available here at tumbleweedhouses.comproducts.htm.

Communities

There are many good examples of small house communities or cottage communities. Here are a few:

- Fairfield, Iowa. Abundance EcoVillage.
- North Shore of Lake Superior, Michigan. Tofte Project, originally founded in 1893.
- Ithica, New York. EcoVillage and home of the Wild Goose Bed & Breakfast Tennessee.
- Washington State. Communities developed by the Cottage Company:
  Bainbridge Island, Washington. Ericksen Cottages, completed 2003.
  Kirkland, Washington. Danielson Grove, completed 2005.
  Redmond, Washington. Conover Commons Cottages, completed 2004.
  Shoreline, Washington. Greenwood Avenue Cottages, completed 2002.
  Whidbey Island, Washington. Backyard Neighborhood, completed 2000 and Third Street Cottages, completed 1998.

Education and Workshops

The information below, describing the organizations, is found on their Web sites.

- Abundance Eco Village. "The idea for the Abundance EcoVillage Project was born of frustration and dissatisfaction with a way of living that is not healthy for the earth or its inhabitants. In a conventional home, subdivision, village, or city, the options provided for energy, water, waste handling, built environment, landscape, food, transportation, and a livelihood are grossly out of tune with the growing desire of many people to live as responsible citizens on the earth, in harmony with our planetary resources and our fellow creature inhabitants."
  Web site: abundance-ecovillage.com

- Association for the Advancement of Sustainability in Higher Education (AASHE). From their Web site, "AASHE is a membership-based association of colleges and universities working to advance sustainability in higher education in the United States and Canada."
  Web site: aashe.org

- Big Green Summer. "Big Green Summer grew out of an informal internship program started in 1998 at Surya Nagar Farm (Iowa and Hawaii—solarfarm.com) and in 2000 at Abundance EcoVillage (Iowa—abundance-ecovillage.com) that has served hundreds of students. This program was developed and directed by Big Green Summer founders Lonnie and Valerie Gamble."
  Web site: biggreensummer.com

- Red Feather Development Group. "I was drawn to Red Feather, because of their hands-on approach. Efforts that emanate from the grass roots are often some of the most effective and creative."
  —Robert Redford
  Web site: redfeather.org

- Root Systems Institute. "Root Systems Institute (RSI) seeks to educate, empower, and inspire people to make sustainable choices that are in alignment with their inner purpose and that support the health of our communities and the planet."
  Web site: rootsystemsinstitute.net

- Solar Farm. "Surya Nagar is Sanskrit for 'Home of the Sun,' and the mission of Surya Nagar is to implement and teach how man can create a life based on solar energy. We operate a farm, offer internships, host visitors, and offer educational programs such as permaculture design certificate courses."
  Web site: solarfarm.com

Designers and Builders

Below is a selection of designers and builders that are fairly well established. These are provided here as a starting point for your own research. All quoted material comes from their Web sites.

- BC Mountain Homes. A wide variety of house plans by John Gower, including some amazingly simple and small houses.
  Web site: bcmountainhomes.com

- BlueSky MOD. "Our approach to manufacturing and materials strikes a balance between what we take from the Earth and how we live on it."
  Web site: blueskymod.com

- DPO Construction. Don Otto built the first 5-Star rated energy efficient home in Iowa.
  Web site: dpoconstruction.com

- Cavco Industries. "We offer a variety of products including Manufactured Homes, Park Model Homes, Camping Cabins, and Commercial Buildings."
  Web site: cavco.com

- Cottage Company. "We're a development and construction company based in Seattle, Washington, and focused on the implementation of 'pocket neighborhoods' of cottages and 'not-so-big' homes."
  Web site: cottagecompany.com

- Creative Cottages. "Designer builder R. McAllister Lloyd, with thirty years of custom-design experience, runs a small Maine company that uses environmentally sensitive building practices to create custom, energy efficient homes in Maine, New Hampshire, and Massachusetts. Combining clients' needs with design knowledge that integrates function and intimacy."
  Web site: creativecottagesllc.com

- Cusato Cottages. "Marianne Cusato founded Cusato Cottages to provide traditional designs for affordable housing."
  Web site: cusatocottages.com

- Insitebuilders. Provider of homes designed by Architect Dennis Fukai, PhD. These steel construction homes are small, cute, modern, and very strong. The Web site provides large photos, basic floor plans, and beautiful 3D model drawings.
  Web site: insitebuilders.com

- Jot-House. "Yeh + Jerrard are the makers of the Jot House—a refreshingly simple, small, and contemporary home design. Through the use of physical and virtual models, Yeh + Jerrard are able to perform lighting analysis and also explore with the client various options for materials and design. This allows the client to be more actively involved in the design process. Yeh + Jerrard are based out of Los Angeles, California."
  Web site: jothouse.com or yehjerrard.com

- Katrina Cottages by Cusato Cottages. "Marianne Cusato founded Cusato Cottages to provide traditional designs for affordable housing."
  Web site: cusatocottages.com

Living Architecture. "We feel it our responsibility to conserve our resources by designing, building and maintaining sustainable structures, developments, towns and cities."
Web site: livingarchitecture.com

m-house. "The m-house is modern, mobile, meticulous, minimalist, and marvelous!"
Web site: m-house.org

Micro Compact Homes (m-ch). "The team of researchers and designers based in London and at the Technical University in Munich developed the m-ch as an answer to an increasing demand for short-stay housing for students, business people, weekenders' sports, and leisure use. The m-ch, now in use and available throughout Europe, combines techniques for high-quality compact living spaces deployed in aircraft, yachts, cars, and micro apartments."
Web site: microcompacthome.com

Mini Cabin Plans. Architect and builder Kevin Meek is the provider of this Web site, which offers unique and inexpensive building plans for low-cost housing.
Web site: minicabinplans.com

Modern Cabana. "A versatile addition designed to accommodate buyers seeking value, modernism, and quality, The Cabana can be used as a guest cottage, a pool house, artist studio, home office, urban penthouse, desert hideaway, fishing cabin, workshop, sound studio, yoga studio, kid's playhouse, or exercise room."
Web site: moderncabana.com

Noble Home. "The housing construction industry is hard on most people. Land is expensive, leaving little money to build one's dream house, not to mention hiring an architect to ensure a livable, inspiring, energy-efficient space. Conversely, affordable rural housing generally consists of uninspired design and inferior quality, and is often a poor investment. Noble Home is a house kit that comes shipped to

your building site and contains all the parts needed to build a finished house shell on your foundation. A kit can save labor costs
because most pieces are cut to size therefore assembly is typically
very fast. Wasted time and money due to incorrect ordering of materials and complex construction is avoided with a kit."
Web site: noble-home.net

➤ Norwester Industries. This group is the provider of custom-built tiny
portable homes.
Web site: norwesterindustries.com

➤ Oasis Design. "Oasis Design is a wellspring of original content and
designs that you won't find elsewhere. We specialize in the nuts and
bolts of sustainability—practical systems for living well, in harmony
with nature and each other. These include designs for managing
water, wastewater, energy, money, and other resources. Our goal is to
live really well, on a small amount of well-managed resources, and
help others do the same. We don't need resource wars . . . we just
need to make the most of our fair share. There are several hundred
pages of free information here on our web site, as well as an additional several hundred in our books and articles. We hope you enjoy your
visit and find something that helps you live the way you want to."
Web site: oasisdesign.net

➤ Rocio Romero Kit Homes. "We design, manufacture, build, ship,
and sell our kit homes. By marrying all these disciplines, we are
able to better deliver quality design easily and affordably. It is
through prefab efficiencies that we are able to control the cost and
quality of our homes."
Web site: rocioromero.com

➤ Ross Chapin Architects. "We are an award-winning firm known for
designing wonderfully scaled and richly detailed buildings and gar-
dens. We take joy in designing places for people that are both functional and beautiful."
Web site: rosschapin.com

- Sanctuary Shelters. Home designer and builder Phil Carson offers "Wildernest Organic Homes" that feature breathing walls and "no-toxic" eco harvested solid wood construction.
  Web site: greencentral.ca

- Sherpa Cabins. "Our goal continues to be to build and deliver the best small cabins in the industry. As we so often hear, 'this cabin is a work of art!' In a world that seems to continually lose its appreciation for quality and craftsmanship we strive to maintain our own in each Sherpa Cabin we build. Sherpa Cabins, Inc., has an engineer-approved structural plan that encompasses each cabin's basic design. Although we have never built two identical cabins, all the cabins have the same general framing. We now have cabins in Idaho, Washington, Colorado, New Mexico, California and Montana."
  Web site: sherpacabins.com

- Structures To Go. Homes you can assemble! Home kits include locally made plywood Structural Insulated Panels (SIPs).
  Web site: structurestogo.com

- Timberlast. This organization's purpose is "to utilize the centuries old technique of timber framing to create truly sustainable structures that will provide strong, aesthetically pleasing shelter for generations to come . . . to build 'small,' in terms of both size and impact."
  —David Fernandez
  Web site: timberlast.com

- Tiny House Company. A small home-builder in the Virginia area.
  Web site: tinyhousecompany.com

- Tiny Texas Houses. "The only 95 percent recycled portable Tiny House on the market in the U.S.A. Yes, there are others who make Tiny Houses, but none who use exclusively vintage lumber and focus on the handmade quality and details of the old days, with original Cypress windows, period doors, hardware, and everything old."
  Web site: discoverys.net/Tiny%20Texas%20Houses.htm

- TreeHouse Company. "TreeHouse Company is the world's largest tree house business and constructs tree houses across the Globe. TreeHouse Company's talented designers create the concepts and craftsmen turn these into reality, building handmade tree houses for children and families."
Web site: treehouse-company.com

- Tropical Treehouse. "The hooch, the ultimate small house, perches on a single point foundation—the smallest footprint of any land-based structure. Radiating anchored cables (to trees, ground, or other natural objects), keep the hooch erect and resilient. With no permanent foundation and zero site alteration, the hooch exemplifies ephemeral architecture, environmental stewardship, and biomimetic design."
Web site: tropical-treehouse.com

- Tumbleweed Tiny House Company. Jay Shafer is one of the first small house designers and builders. He is considered by many to be an authority on the small house movement. His artistic and efficient designs have won various awards.
Web site: tumbleweedhouses.com

- V2World. "Dedicated to building environmentally respectful residential and commercial spaces that are assembled through an efficient and repetitive process. By using a steel framing system of stackable modules, numerous configurations are possible."
Web site: v2world.net

- Ventura Prefab Homes. "Offering pre-cut homes made from the finest Brazilian hardwoods, the wood arrives at your building site ready for immediate assembly. Your home or cabin can be provided with double wall construction and extra insulation for cold climates, and the roof can be constructed to support heavy loads of snow. Available are simple one-bedroom cabins of 375 square feet. Prices start at around $15,000. Buyers may choose to purchase just the complete wood kit and install the bathroom and kitchen fixtures from local sources, or opt for the finishing kit."
Web site: venturaprefabhomes.com

➤ Vermont Tiny House. "Although their houses are tiny, they are fully functional, fully finished, and range from $10,000 to $22,000. The smaller models come with sleeping loft, and the larger models include a floor-level sleeping area. They're insulated and can be wired for AC (on-grid) or DC (off-grid) power. They are fully able to accommodate solar or other alternative power sources."
Web site: vermonttinyhouse.com

➤ weeHouses by Alchemy Architects. "The mission of Alchemy Architects is to make stimulating, engaging, and efficient design accessible and affordable to a wide audience. Their distinctive hands-on approach to architecture and design combines a playful design process, collaborative relationships with clients, and partnerships with builders and fabricators, to create a harmonious blend of site, building, and community."
Web site: weehouses.com

Publications

The small house movement has resulted in numerous publications. Here is an abbreviated list of the Web sites associated with some of them:

CabinLife.com
CottageLife.com
CottageLiving.com
CottageMagazine.com
HomesAndCottages.com
NorthernHomeAndCottage.com
TheLastStraw.org

Small House Plans

In addition to the house plans offered by the designers and builders listed previously, there are also Web sites that offer house plans. These sites are provided without any guarantee of quality but are simply a starting point for your own reference and research. Most of these sites offer the option of searching by size, so it's possible to find just the right size house plan that you desire.

ArchitecturalDesigns.com
ArchitecturalHousePlans.com
CoolHousePlans.com
DreamHomeSource.com
eHousePlans.com
ePlans.com
GlobalHousePlans.com
HomePlans.com
HousePlanGallery.com
HousePlanGuys.com
HousePlans.com
HousePlans.ca (Canada)
PlanHouse.com
RossChapin.com
TheHouseDesigners.com
ThePlanCollection.com
TinyHomes.com
TumbleweedHouses.com
UltimatePlans.com
WeinMaster.com (Canada)

Online Tools for Smaller Living

Here are some online resources for living well in smaller spaces, including small houses and small apartments. If your small space needs a makeover, these are the resources to help you declutter your life:

- ApartmentTherapy.com—Great resource for living well and living small.
- CoolHousePlans.com—Excellent resource for small house plans.
- Curbly.com—Excellent online resource for interior design and do-it-yourself advice.
- DecorNextDoor.com
- Plan3D.com—Design your home or living space in 3D online or using this software on your computer.

Additional Resources

Below are other useful online resources for living in greater health, wellness, and simplicity:

Cdc.gov/HealthyLiving
LowImpactLiving.com
WebMd.com/a-to-z-guides/healthy-living

Author Bio

GREGORY PAUL JOHNSON is the founder and director of Resources for Life, an outreach and public interest organization based in Iowa City, Iowa. His small home, the Mobile Hermitage, has received significant worldwide media attention, and his study of Urban and Regional Planning with the Higher Education Consortium for Urban Affairs (HECUA) included travel to Panama, Colombia, Ecuador, and Peru. Today, as a technology consultant, Gregory works for the University of Iowa as well as for clients served by his consulting firm, the Technology Services Resource Group. For more information on Gregory, go to the Web site Resourcesfor Life.com.